Copyright © 2015 Charlotte Howard - Heart Centered Women Media.

All rights reserved. No part of this publication may be reproduced, distributed or transmitted in any form or by any means, including photocopying, recording, or other electronic or mechanical methods, without the prior written permission of the publisher, except in the case of brief quotations embodied in critical reviews and certain other noncommercial uses permitted by copyright law. For permission requests, write to the publisher, addressed "Attention: Permissions Coordinator," at the address below.

Charlotte Howard - Heart Centered Women Media

108 Flintlock Lane

Summerville, SC/USA 29486

www.heartcenteredwomenpublishing.com

charlotte@thehairartistassociation.org

Book Cover ©2015 Charlotte Howard - Heart Centered Women Media

Book Layout ©2015 Charlotte Howard - Heart Centered Women Media

Compiled By Charlotte Howard & Daija Howard - Heart Centered Women Media

Ordering Information:

Quantity sales. Special discounts are available on quantity purchases by corporations, associations, and others. For details, contact the "Special Sales Department" at the address above.

Roar: The Confidence to Heal Your Heart, Create True Beauty and Empower Women by Charlotte Howard and Daija Howard. —1st ed.

ISBN-13: 978-0692588093

ASIN: 0692588094

Table of Contents

Preface 3
Confidence 5
Do you have what it takes to be confident? 14
Controlling your Beliefs 18
How to overcome Negative Thoughts 24
How to feel Confident all the time 45
Life 51
How to lead a Confident Life 52
Mapping Out What You Want in Your Life 63
Fire The Gun! – How to Take Action 67
Overcoming Problems and Difficulties 80
How to Keep Motivated and Make the Changes 87
How to Live The Life You Want 91
Business 122
Plan Your Best Year Ever With Confidence 123
   REVIEW & CELEBRATE THE PAST 12 MONTHS 123
   UNDERSTANDING YOUR 'WHY' 127
   YOUR BUSINESS VISION 129
   GOAL SETTING 130
   BREAKING IT DOWN: YOUR YEAR AT
   A GLANCE 132
   CREATE DO-ABLE TASKS 133
   RESOURCES I NEED 134
   ACCOUNTABILITY & SUPPORT 135
   A LIVING DOCUMENT 136

Preface

"Your attitude determines your altitude. It really is true that if you think you can, you can; and if you think you can't, you're right.

In today's world that so strongly emphasizes the importance of self-confidence, the modern woman has no choice but to spruce up her confidence levels or she'll be left far behind in the rat race and never be able to rise above it.

Roar: The Confidence to Heal Your Heart, Create True Beauty and Empower Women will help you improve on and raise those confidence levels in all areas of your life and business just the way you want.

Through **Roar: The Confidence to Heal Your Heart, Create True Beauty and Empower Women** you will participate in extraordinary exercises and assignments, which are more than just learning experiences.

Roar: The Confidence to Heal Your Heart, Create True Beauty and Empower Women will help you break through all barriers and fixed notions you have about yourself, life and business.

Confident women are successful women. Women stick it out until they get what they want. This is because women confidently believe in their goals and their own ability.

If you are reading this now, you are aware that a lack of confidence has seriously held you back in achieving the important goals of your life and business. We dedicate this book to you. It is time you do away with your misgivings and lack of self-belief.

You don't want to be timid and quiet when the women around you are confident and brimming with life, do you? So, fight the shyness and get what you want – SELF CONFIDENCE! The authentic kind that you are destined to have.

To your success,

Charlotte Howard
#1 International Best Selling Author, Publisher and Beauty Transformational Life Coach

Confidence

Reprogramming the confident woman from within

The strong confident woman we all admire her, said Sharon Nicholas. We wonder how she became who she is today. We wonder who she is and how she became so confident. We wonder what her background has been like to have fostered such a high level of confidence.

Have you ever seen such a women like this at an event or speaking engagement and wondered who she is? Only later once you meet her, you learn she was the victim of domestic abuse or grew up as a neglected child. How does someone come off that confident having come from such circumstances? How has she emerged with high self-esteem and self-confidence? Not everyone would emerge with their self-esteem intact. How is she different? What was it about her that she was able to develop such confidence?

For many of us, the lack of self-esteem or a positive self-image has plagued us from the time we are young. People are naturally different, extroverts are born more confident. Introverts are not as naturally confident, but confidence is something which can be built. Another cause of lower self-esteem is simply our personality. Some of us are very shy by nature. We're more introverted and less self-confident not through any fault of our own, just by personality type. Some of us are not as self-confident. It's nature not nurture. This lower level of self-confidence has not been the result of anything which has happened to us.

It's a fact, having great self-confidence is not natural for everyone. Many of us have spent lifetime building and working on our self-esteem and confidence. We as women are so bombarded with negativity derived from so many different sources. Negativity comes from our family, friends, personal relationships, school settings, the workplace and the media. No wonder self-confidence for many is a lifelong struggle. Regardless if you came from a supportive community or not. Self-esteem and self-confidence are a struggle for many women. You can also have periods in your life where you have a health sense of self-esteem then struggle. You may struggle with self-esteem and self-confidence at other times of your life.

Some of us are lucky to have strong family support and a supportive group of friends who work to cultivate our self-confidence and help a build positive self-worth within us. Some of us are blessed with strong communities surrounding us with positivity. Being surrounded by a positive and productive community creates positive thinking within us and is the cornerstone of mental health. When our interactions are kind and giving with others, these positive interactions with others are turned into our self-thoughts we reflect on. These thoughts are either in our conscious or subconscious mind. Once you realize the importance of your community and the impact your community has on your thoughts, reflect on your own community and how it influences you.

Sadly, others of us are not so blessed to have a strong community. We lack the positive interactions to flourish positive thinking within us. Some of us have had to learn to build our self-esteem and self-confidence by ourselves. Without a strong community assisting you along the way, sometimes you'll end up doing the work yourself by seeking a professional counselor to help you.

Give thought to how your community impacts your thoughts. Especially if your community is a negative one, rethink your community and change your environment. You must do the self-work regardless to improve your self-esteem and confidence.

Some of us have had good self-esteem, but from negative life events our self-esteem and self-confidence has been shattered. Hard life events such as loss of a job or divorce can really take a toll on even the most confident person. These events can create havoc on one's self-esteem and self-confidence. Many times when a personal relationship breaks up or if we've been bullied in the workplace or in a school setting it can have a direct impact on our self-esteem and self-confidence.

Are you someone who has been through any of these life events such as the loss of a marriage or job loss? Do you feel your self-esteem and self-confidence have been impacted? To really understand the difference between self-esteem and self-confidence, let's break it down.

Self-esteem refers to how you feel about yourself overall. How much self-esteem or positive regard or self-love you have. Self-esteem develops from experiences and situations that have shaped how you view yourself today and it is built by both external and internal forces.

Self-confidence is how you feel about your abilities and can vary from situation to situation and time to time. You may be perfectly confident in one area of knowledge or skillset but may lack self-confidence in another area.

You may have healthy self-esteem, but low confidence about situations involving public speaking or being on stage. Someone who has very high level of self-confidence may be comfortable in both situations. This level of self-confidence may have been built over many years. Keep in mind the shyest of us can build confidence. They may not have always had this level of self-confidence.

Many circumstances can have a direct impact on our self-esteem and self-confidence. Many circumstances not by our own choosing can have a negative result on our lives. For example, the person you ended up with for a boss is not within your control. It can directly impact your self-esteem and self-confidence if you have a negative or abusive boss.

We have all had negative controlling bosses in our careers. Bosses who manipulate the work place, who delegate their responsibilities to others, who fail to connect with their employees and seem to enjoy excluding some employees. We've all had bosses who play the favoritism card and purposely make the workplace difficult by being negative in the workplace. We never forget the ones who routinely make negative comments.

How to help yourself, when you are presented with this type of negative situation which could harm you? First, you must take charge of your thoughts. Implement strategies to help you through, use your own positive self-talk. Work on your own self-chatter. Do not internalize what a negative person has to say. Recognize from whom the comments are coming from. Your opinion of yourself is far more important than any outsider. Value your own opinions higher.

Ultimately when you love yourself, your self-esteem improves and makes you more confident. A higher self-esteem has a way of building confidence within us. When you are confident in some areas of your life, your talents and skills, you begin to increase your overall sense of self-esteem. One really reinforces the other and you can work on developing both.

Often not feeling good enough or worthy comes from unhealthy relationships throughout life. The relationships we have with our parents, siblings, extended family, classmates, friends, co-workers, bosses and personal relationships all have an effect on our self-esteem and confidence. This concept of self has developed over our entire life. Your self-image is on a continuum and changes from time to time depending on your thinking. Internalized thoughts and feelings reflect on our own self-image. Self-image and self-worth are key to feeling good about yourself.

Healthy relationships have a way of building our self-confidence and self-esteem while negative relationships teardown our self-esteem then our self-confidence slides. In relationships which where we are belittled or ripped down by our family members, friends, classmates, bosses or our loved ones were we are constantly told negative things directly impacts our thinking.

Words can hurt us on such a deep level, far more than we are even aware of. Often when someone else says something negative we will dwell on these words for weeks or maybe even years later. If the harsh words were from a significant relationship these words can linger a lifetime. This negative script does impact the way we view ourselves, our self-esteem and self-confidence are directly tied to the negative and hateful words of others.

On the positive side, in areas you are confident about your talents such as being a good friend or terrific parent can build your confidence. If you focus on your strengths it helps your self-image, self-worth and confidence. Know and trust your true strengths in areas you feel confident in.

Those areas will build your self-confidence ultimately. Staying focused on your personal strengths will build your self-esteem and self-confidence back up. Areas you are confident in should be your main focus at the times you're struggling with your self-esteem. Working on changing negative self-talk, self-doubts and lack of confidence is something which can be changed; it's not a permanent condition.

Know that respect for oneself is as important as respect for others. Low self-esteem is tied to respect for self. Caring for yourself will help build your self-esteem back up. We as women are so focused on caring for those around us we often for get to care for ourselves. All of our time and energy is focused on helping those around us. Time and energy is required to help you sometimes instead of helping others. Know that simple things can boost your confidence take the steps and improve your view of yourself.

When someone makes a negative comment which hurts you we all have a tendency to internalize the comments of others. Know that is only their perception of you, you know yourself better than anyone does. Don't let the insults or negative comments of others impact your view of yourself. Why let the perception of another person directly influence your life? Perceptions are not always right and often are exaggerated for impact.

Perceptions are beliefs, judgements and emotions set to words which are not always based on fact. Often the reason someone is making negative comments and directing them on you is because they themselves don't feel good about themselves. Your self-worth is about you; do not base your self-esteem on biased and perceived comments by negative people.

Tips for self-esteem and self-confidence:

- Stop the negative self-chatter in your own head. Much of our own negative thinking has come from others comments. Ease these "I can't" or "I'm not good enough" type statements. Replace your self-chatter with "I am working on" and "I am building and improving" type of statements.
- Daily mantras and affirmations will help you connect with your new direction and your new thinking about your life.
- Daily gratitude journals all help to reconnect with yourself with what you value about yourself.
- Focusing on your strengths first once you have mastered an area or a skill this will build your self-confidence.
- Make list of all of you good qualities and things you like about yourself. Self-love and appreciating yourself is key to having good self-esteem.
- As soon as a negative thought comments to mind rebuttal it with a positive thought.
- Think of qualities others say you excel in. Even if you believe them slightly, embrace the thoughts.
- Be as kind to yourself as you are to others. Stop saying these negative statements to yourself which you would not say to another person.
- Know that everyone has negative self-chatter from time to time but it's not something you cannot work on to improve.
- Make a list of your personal, professional strengths and achievements. Think of what others would say about you if they were with you right now.
- If you have tried many techniques to overcome your low self-esteem and nothing has worked seek out counseling.

- Volunteering is a great way to build your self-esteem. Helping others takes you r mind off of yourself.
- Work on changing your mind-set.
- Failures are moments were we learn and grow.
- Change your circle of friends if they are not positive thinkers and have a positive influence on your mind. A housecleaning may be in order.
- Work on your thoughts daily. Reflect on positive thinking and new changes in your life.

More tips for self-esteem and self-confidence:

- Focus on your strengths and not your weaknesses.
- Do one small good dead per day.
- Learn to value your own opinions of yourself higher than others' opinions of you.
- Develop your own inner peace as your own refuge from the world.
- Take care of yourself. Exercise, eat right and get enough sleep. All have a direct impact on how you feel about yourself.
- Don't feel guilty about ever investing in yourself.
- Changing your job or your environment will improve your thoughts.
- Spend time outside with nature and reconnect with Mother Nature.
- Don't compare your life to others. You are your own individual.
- Embrace your successes and don't focus on your failures.
- Visit old friends and family members you don't see much of.
- Create new positive habits to improve your life.
- Take up new hobbies.

The more we recognize and accept our own challenges with self-confidence and self-esteem the more we can do something about it.

We can make positive life improvements to work on both concerns. Becoming more aware of your own self-doubts and negative self-chatter is the start. Being aware is the first step before a positive change can occur.

To your success,

Sharon Nicholas

Do you have what it takes to be confident?

Take the assessment and all will be revealed!

During my last year in high school I got pregnant with my oldest daughter. It devastated my mom. In fact she told me I wouldn't finish high school, I wouldn't go to cosmetology school, I wouldn't graduate cosmetology school and I wouldn't ever amount to anything in life. I felt hopeless with my mom telling me this but because I began personal development, my life changed.

I was diagnosed with carpal tunnel syndrome back in the year 2000 after working 80 hours a week as a beauty salon manager. My supervisor literally handed my job over to the next person in line and I had to train that person to be as good as I was after taking multiple salons to six-figures.

My life and perspectives changed once I met many women mentors like Pam Perry, Lashanda Henry and Ann Sieg who inspired me to want more and be more, I was able to turn my life around. Because of magazines like Oprah and books like think and grow rich I began to boost my confidence implementing what I learned. I began to inspire others through writing books, hosting events and inspirational platforms for others to share their voice, said Charlotte Howard.

I'm not the only woman who have faced confidence challenges.

Alexis Hart was a member of a women spirituality group at her church. At 43, she was shy to speak up with friends, or in groups. During a convention on seniors activity group Alexis was unexpectedly asked to speak to the members. After the initial panic and fear, she slowly found herself relaxing. Deep breaths and pep talk on the way to the pulpit worked! She was finally able to give an anxiety-free talk to the group.

Alexis Hart was taking a boost your confidence building workshop at the time and was 2 weeks into it.

Or let's take the case of Natasha Hyatt. 24 year old Natasha was a skilled graphic designer and though her resume exhibited her credentials, she could never really voice them. Since most jobs required her to interact with clients, she failed to make an impression on prospective employers due to her lack of communication skills and self-confidence. Luckily, Natasha enrolled herself in a boost your confidence building workshop and within a few weeks got through an interview at an international firm.

Now isn't that a very positive note to start a Boost Your Confidence Building platform?

You agree?

Great!

This chapter is all about self-discovery. Unless you know where you are, how will you move to where you want to be?

Before we begin boost your confidence building exercises that will work on areas where you need more confidence, take the assessment test below, said Charlotte Howard.

****
Self-assessment
****

Rate the following statements from 0 – 10 based on how much you believe each of them to be true.

- ➢ 0 would mean that you don't believe in the statement at all and that it's utter nonsense.

- ➢ 10 would mean you think it's completely true.

****

Statements
****

- I like myself as a person
- I am as good as everyone else
- When I look at myself in the mirror I like what I see
- I don't feel like an overall failure
- I am happy to be me
- I respect myself
- I'd rather be me than anyone else
- What others say to me has no affect
- I enjoy communicating to others
- I have the skills and qualities to make myself a success
- I like to take risks
- I am not afraid to make mistakes
- I can laugh at myself

Now sum up all your scores.

Want to know where your confidence level stands?
Here goes...

If you have scored:

100 – 130

You have a high level of self esteem and confidence. All you have to do is fine tune it and increase your confidence in a couple of areas.

65 – 99

You have a medium to high ranking in self esteem. Whilst most of the time you are okay, there are times when you can feel rock bottom. You need more consistent feelings that you are confident and learn to experience these more regularly.

30 – 64

You have low levels of self esteem.

You lack confidence in yourself in most areas and need to have an overall confidence building plan.

0 – 29

You have reached rock bottom and think that everything and everyone is against you. You are stuck in a rut and need to get out of it quick

So, what are your scores like? Are they satisfactory, or are you hiding them under the couch?

Hold it, if you are! There's nothing to hide or feel ashamed about.

What you could do is write down some of the observations you made along this assessment.

What do you specifically need to concentrate on with regards to building up your confidence?

It is not in every area of your life where you need confidence, only some.

Please get these down – the first step to improving anything is knowing where you are currently at.

Okay, so that's it for this chapter.

Controlling your Beliefs

Have you completed the assessment test by now said Sonya Davis?

What were your scores like?

What you can do now is write down what 2 things you would love to master with regards to your confidence.

With the upcoming exercise you will begin to create the person that you want to become in terms of confidence.

The secret of success here lies in a visual image of how you would want to act, walk, talk, think and move your body so that you know what to aspire for.

Remember that we are working with confidence set your goal! ☐

And like any other goal you want to achieve, this one too should be clear because you should know what you are after and how you are going to get it.

The next step to confidence is if your self-esteem reaches rock bottom, what should you do? Think of your CONFIDENCE ROLE MODEL and ask yourself:

"How would my confidence role model deal with this situation?"

When you have your answer, do just as your role model did. This might feel weird in the beginning, but it will do you loads of good.

PRACTICAL

Moving on, there must be a woman whose confidence levels you admire a lot; a mentor, coach, colleague, friend, someone in your family or even a famous personality who oozes self-confidence; someone who has high self-esteem and therefore you admire.

Think about this person if you would like your confidence levels to boost up just like her.

On the other hand, this is your chance to start from scratch- to improve the way you walk, talk, and think; and your body language on the whole.

Ponder, ponder, ponder; long and hard.

You have to now fill out the following sections. Make sure the person whose confidence levels you admire is really worth admiration.

MY CONFIDENCE ROLE MODEL

She would act like…

She would talk like…

She would walk like…

She would think like…

Her body language would be like…

Other people think that she is…

When faced with problems, she thinks…

Now take note of the few things you have written down about your confidence role model. The idea is to make an effort to be like you desire to be. So let's start with the basics.

Put these qualities into action. Yes! You heard it right.

<u>ACT AS IF YOU ARE THE WOMAN YOU WANT TO BE AND NOTICE THE RESULTS.</u>

Don't worry if this feels awkward, because it will! After all you are acting out what you are really not. It will take a while for it to sink within and feel normal.

You will also need a strong inner belief system to be the confident woman you want to become. Self-acceptance gives you the much needed energy and room to grow. Your inner belief system helps you develop an ability to accept yourself – who we are, what we feel, think and do.

The benefits of a strong inner belief system are varied and great:

- Stronger self confidence
- Healthy self esteem
- Greater life satisfaction
- Comfort with self and others

How is this inner belief system developed, said Charlotte Howard?

Consider the following questions. Finding the answers to these can help you to weed out the **mess** of what "everybody else says" and get back to the purity and perfection of self-expression.

1. **What are your current beliefs about work, life, people, and about yourself? Let go and try a free-writing exercise.**
    - On top of a page write one word (work, life, etc, - one for each page) and then free associate for each word.

- Write down whatever thoughts might be conjured up by the word at the top of the page.
- Write until each page is full!

2. How much of what you believe is your own?

- Take a look at what you wrote on each page.
- What messages may have come from parents, friends, family, peers, teachers, etc?
- Identify the recurring themes?
- Now, pick out and highlight the things you feel truly reflect who you are and what you believe.

3. How much of it is enabling versus disabling?

- Are the messages that came from others enabling and empowering? Or are they limiting?
- Now, look at the ones that reflect your own inner belief system-are those empowering or limiting?
- How do they make you feel?

4. What do you want to believe?

- Ponder over your true beliefs.
- Do they reflect how you want to feel about life, work, people and yourself?
- Write each idea or thought down on the left hand side of a page, and on the right hand side, write how you'd like to feel/think about each instead.
- Reprogram yourself by identifying these limiting thoughts as they pop into your head, and replacing them with the thoughts and ideas you identified on the right hand side instead.

- If you continue this exercise, you'll find the old limiting thoughts creeping up less and less, and the new empowering thoughts will begin to take their place.

5. What messages about life, people, work and yourself did you get from family as you shaped your personality?

- Be prepared.
- Messages from family members are repetitive and will keep coming up.
- If you have chosen to reprogram any of their thoughts, values and beliefs, then be prepared to counter these beliefs whenever a family member articulates them.

6. What's your response when you express your belief and someone disagrees?

- How are you going to respond should you share your beliefs with others, and find that they disagree?
- Here's a hint: don't change your mind. It's okay that someone else believes differently from you-that's what makes the world go round after all.
- Instead, simply state that you see life/work/people/etc. differently, and then repeat and reconfirm your belief to yourself.

These questions, their answers and the exercises associated with each are sure to strengthen your belief system. Just like your soul that gives you life, you don't have to reinforce or communicate your belief. Nevertheless its presence is undisputed.

Your challenge is to develop confidence in your ability to express these beliefs in an unwavering fashion.

There are people who will disregard your beliefs. What you have to do is test your ability to continue with your belief system and keep it intact as a part of your personal growth. If it continues to feel solid, then restate and reinforce it strongly.

Moving ahead, in the process, once your belief system has been strengthened, you will find that those having less confidence in their own beliefs will seek you out.

You can now help and encourage others and tap them into your own belief system, following the process you used to get where you are now.

Well then, what are you waiting for?

Start now!

How to overcome Negative Thoughts

Even the most positive woman get negative thoughts, said Daija Howard!

Yes, that's true.

Music Icon, Beyonce Knowles Carter during her performance, said she lost focus by nurturing negative thoughts on why she was given her talent. Knowles Carter confessed that though she had convinced herself that it was meant for her.

Actually, negative thoughts are commonplace and any woman can be a 'victim' to them. However, it's not the presence of negative thoughts but the way we handle and react to them that either breaks or makes our confidence and self-esteem.

Think over this:

NOTHING HAS ANY MEANING IN LIFE, ONLY THE MEANING YOU GIVE TO IT.

If you ALLOW negative thoughts to HARM you – THEY WILL!

If you ALLOW negative thoughts to HELP you – THEY WILL!

Before we get into this next chapter it's important to keep a few points in mind:

- It's not only you that gets negative thoughts; every woman on this planet gets them.
- You are not making an attempt to uproot negative thoughts here. Just handling them more smartly.

- Negative thoughts, as such, do not harm you. It's what you say to yourself after the thought has entered your head that harms you.
- You can change any thought you want by changing what it means to you.

With that taken into account, let's kick off this next chapter!

Analyzing your thoughts

Want to increase your confidence? You have to first find out what triggers off those negative thoughts and emotions you have about yourself.

It becomes easier to analyze and respond to them if you write them down.

FYI, it is not the trigger or the event that instigates the bad feelings. What make you feel despondent are the internal dialogues you say to yourself in response to the trigger.
These catalysts distort reality and put your feelings in turmoil.

That's the kind of turmoil Lynette got into. Her husband Roger had been quite distracted over the past few days. Lynette tried talking to him on a couple of occasions but he wasn't forthcoming. She heard him talking in hushed tones over the phone, and he also came home late more often than before. Lynette was perturbed beyond words. She spent hours talking to herself, wondering what Roger was up to.

She would have said:

- **"He's ignoring me."**
- **"Maybe he's having an affair with someone."**
- **"He doesn't find me attractive or interesting anymore."**

What would she have felt?

- **Anger**
- **Resentment**
- **Grief**
- **Self-pity**

Maybe she should have been more probing; or given more time to her husband. Did she know her husband well enough to arrive at these conclusions?

In fact Roger must have been having a tough time at work. A bad review by the boss, a fall in profits in business, tiff with a colleague. It could have been anything!

The point is nothing in life has any meaning, only the meaning you give it.

Roger must have had a completely unconnected problem, but to Lynette it looked like a problem in their relationship!

Controlling your inner voice and what you say to yourself either makes or breaks your self-esteem and confidence.

Within this session, you will be introduced to a technique, which you can use to control your inner dialogue and to make you appraise just how hard and unreasonable you are on yourself.

But before we get into the exercise, let's just discuss those negative thoughts you have.

Here's a small little recap – *It is not the trigger or the event that instigates the bad feelings. But the internal dialogues you say to yourself in response to the trigger that makes you despondent.*

Okay, to make it easier to understand, let's split these negative thoughts or distortions into 13 categories.

Here's the list. You can use this as a quick reference:

1. **Assuming**
2. **Over-generalising**
3. **'Shoulds'**
4. **Labeling**
5. **Binning the positives**
6. **And they all lived happily ever after**

7. **Blaming other people and events**
8. **It's all or nothing!**
9. **Negative thinking erodes your soul!**
10. **Believing what you feel**
11. **Personalizing**
12. **Making comparisons with others**
13. **I can't cope with life**

While we go through them one by one, make notes of the ones you use most frequently.

1. Assuming

When you make assumptions with your thinking, you are assuming the worst without knowing the full picture or without testing the evidence.

Let's go back to our example about Lynette and her husband. She didn't have any of the facts; she just assumed that her relationship with her husband was in deep trouble.

She could have tested the assumption by going up to him and saying "Roger, did I do something that upset you? What's wrong? I think we should talk this out."

Other examples of assuming self-talk are:

- "I know this project is going to be rubbish"
- "I know I'll make loads of mistakes if I'm best man"
- "I know people will just hate me"

How could you rephrase some of these thoughts above to make them more realistic? Example – "I am going to give this project a chance and make up my own mind."

2. Over-generalizing

This is when you over-generalize your thoughts and make them more intense by the words you use.

For instance, you would say things like:

- **"I always end up on the losing side."**
- **"I make mistakes in everything I do."**
- **"Everyone hates me."**
- **"Everyone thinks I am so dumb."**
- **"I never do any good at cooking."**

Even when you read these lines their demoralizing effect is so evident!

As much as you know that such over-generalizing internal dialogues are inaccurate, unjust and unfair and affect your confidence, yet you use them.

You certainly are not making mistakes in everything you do?!

You think you are making a mistake right now?

It's not everything that you do then, is it?

How do you turn this around?

Well, a better phrase to use would be, "Sometimes my cooking doesn't turn out very well but overall I am a good cook."

Look for the good in situations and what is working well. It can do wonders!

3. 'Shoulds'

Some people surround themselves with 'Shoulds'.

- "I should be thinner."
- "I should have more friends."
- "I should be earning more money."

Are you the kind who says 'should' all the time?

'Shoulds' are the demands you place on yourself.

A 'should' represents what you are not doing but you think you should be!

So when you know you 'should' be doing something but are not doing it, how do you feel?

Inadequate, hopeless, frustrated? Yes, the list can go on.

So, what are your plans to get rid of the 'shoulds'?

It's easy. Just change the 'should' to 'want' or 'could'.

- "I want to do this"
- "How could I do this?"

4. Labeling

How often do you use an adjective to describe yourself?

Labeling is a common syndrome. This is when you give yourself a name or statement that describes who you are.

For example:

- "I am a loser."
- "I am stupid."
- "I am ugly."
- "I am fat."

How is it possible that you are a loser in every aspect of your life? Is there nothing in you that is attractive? Are you forever a dimwit?

Of course not!

Stop labeling yourself and be specific in your thoughts.

Instead of saying "I am a loser" say "That didn't work out how I would have liked."

5. Binning the positives

Do you tend to overlook the compliments people give you?

Do you refuse to accept and ignore if someone says "That was a great job, well done" or "You look fantastic today"?

How do you usually reply to praise?

"Oh, it was nothing, it was easy" or "I don't look great really, you're just saying that."

Do you realize that you've just discounted the fact that you worked really hard to get that job done or that you take time over your appearance to get it right?

Let's set this record straight. A simple "Thank you" with a smile is the perfect response.

Think it over. Is it that much of an effort?

You would give credit to someone who did a great job. Make sure you accept the credit when you do a great job or when you receive a compliment.

6. And they all lived happily ever after

Perfection is an illusion.

Oh yes it is. No point arguing here.

So if you are a person who has to have everything perfect in your life, it's going to be pretty tough, buddy! You are setting yourself up for disappointments.

Do you have thoughts like:

- "That shouldn't happen to me."
- "I can't believe that has happened."
- "That's unfair."

Stop looking for that perfect world. Everyone has things happen to him or her, good and bad. You are not a special case and no one is exempt.

Instead accept that bad times fall on all and ask yourself "What could I do to improve this situation now?"

7. Blaming other people and events

Do you blame others and don't accept responsibility for outcomes that are different from your expectations?

Do you say?

- "If only my parents had been more ambitious I'd have had more success by now."
- "If only I didn't have to impress all of the time."
- "He makes me feel so bad."
- "She had a hold over me which means I can't do anything."

While this attitude is awful, it will also make you feel like a 'victim'. Forever you will move ahead with a sense of helplessness; that you are capable of nothing.

It isn't your fault. Is it?

YES, IT IS!

Agreed, the event has had an effect on you but at the end of the day only you have the responsibility to let it affect you.

So, how do you turn these thoughts around?

Well, for starters, focus on the reality.

If you feel something is unfair or unjust, accept that it is.

Then accept that the impact it has on you is your responsibility.

Don't make excuses; it is your responsibility!

8. it's all or nothing!

There's more than just black and white. There are several colors in between, right? Like blue, green, red, yellow, pink, brown, purple, mauve…phew!

Then why are most aspects of life just black or white? Are you one of those who think "It's all or nothing"?

Is there no grey area in between?!

- **"I am either a success or a failure."**
- **"If I get first place, I am a winner. If I get second place, I am a loser", irrespective if there are 20,000 runners!**
- **"If I don't get things 100% perfect I am a flop."**
- **"If I don't get an A Grade in Math, I am a failure."**

Well, in life there are rarely successes and failures. In fact, success is a journey, not a destination.

Success and failure are not meant to be measured on a 100 or 0 scale. At the end of the day if you don't perform to your highest standards, it certainly doesn't mean you scored a zero!

Your "It's all or nothing" thought is only setting you up for failures.

How many times do you perform with absolute perfection?

Less than 10% of the time!

So, does that mean you are a failure 90% of the time?
Now you know that's utter nonsense.

Why so you always have to be perfect?

9. **Negative thinking erodes your soul!**

How do you react to events that don't work out the way you planned?

Negatively?

For instance, your boss has said that you completed a piece of work incorrectly, so you say to your partner that you have had a terrible day.

You may have burnt the pie, so the whole meal is ruined.

You might have cut your finger while hiking so the entire holiday is messed up.

Your thought makes the entire situation negative.

What happens if you change your focus when you start thinking negatively?

You can say:
- **"What is still good about this situation?"**
- **"That is only one bad thing, what are the good things?"**
- **"What could I still enjoy about this experience?"**

10. **Believing what you feel**

Feelings are not facts. If you believe your feelings blindly, just too bad, my friend. Mend your ways or you are sure to suffer a confidence setback.

The quality of your life is based upon the quality of your feelings.

Feelings are only thoughts that we have decided to generate. That doesn't make them real.

You give meaning to your thoughts; and hence your feelings.

So, are you the type of woman who believes all the feelings you have?

- "I feel bad. Therefore, I must be bad."
- "I feel like a loser. Therefore, I must be a loser."
- "I feel ugly. Therefore, I must be ugly."

Low levels of confidence can distort your thoughts. So you really need to question your feelings before you believe them.

Ask yourself questions like:

- "What would someone who is a 100% loser, is bad or ugly be like?"
- "Am I really like that?"

Challenge your feelings by questioning them.

11. Personalizing

Personalizing is when you blame yourself.

Personalizing happens when you say:

- "It's entirely my fault that my son didn't get the chances in life."
- "If I wasn't so clingy, men would stay with me."
- "It's all my fault that we got divorced."

Blaming yourself for others actions and decision means you are taking too many responsibilities on your shoulders.

Don't!

Simply because you are not accountable for someone else's decision-making.

Remember that you are not the only one giving advice or offering opinions. An individual meets numerous people and hence gets a number of opinions. But in the end he or she has the freedom to decide what he or she wants to do.

Agreed mistakes do happen and some of them could be the result of your action or decision. But all of them?! You don't believe that, do you?

Your confidence is suffering a blow every time you hold yourself liable for someone else's life turning out to be miserable.

Take the reigns of your life into your hands. Don't blame yourself and don't let others do it unjustly.

12. **Making comparisons with others**

Do you always compare yourself to others?

If you do, it's high time you stop.

Why are you putting yourself through so much of worthless competition? Frankly, it isn't even healthy competition.

What you are doing through such a comparison is magnify your 'weaknesses' and others' 'strengths' or shrink others' 'weaknesses' and your 'strengths'.

So, are you saying something like this?

- "I haven't got a chance for this job, after all who is going to want to hire a single Mom? Charlotte is young, single and she has got a degree."
- "I am hopeless at spelling and math, Mariah is great at these, she can do them standing on her head."
- "No-one will want to go out with me; I've got a big nose. Look at Donna. She is beautiful, has lovely hair and really nice skin."

Challenge these thoughts!

Appreciate that you are a unique person and stop these distortions.

13. I can't cope with life

If you find yourself saying stuff like:

- "I can't stand it."
- "I couldn't live without you."
- "I can manage this."

So what are you doing? Accepting defeat and telling yourself that you are not strong enough to cope with life?

Yes, a lot of things in life are unpleasant, difficult and not nice.

But you can cope with it!

A better way of saying something is:

- "I don't really like this but I can stand it."

How do you challenge and question this thinking? By asking the following:

- "If this does happen, will I really be helpless and be unable to cope?"
- "If the worst happens, what will I do?"
- "When I look back in 30 years' time, will anyone really care about this?"

How to overcome Negative Comments from others

Nothing has any meaning in life, only the meaning you give to it, said Charlotte Howard.

You've heard that before, haven't you? How far have you come to believe in it?

It's not what people say to you that is a problem. People talk! Yes, they do, and there is nothing you can do to stop them. However, it's what you say to yourself after people say something unpleasant that leads to a problem.

Are you left behind with a feeling of dejection?

Let's tackle that feeling, and banish it from our lives!

How to respond to confidence destroyers

Like we discussed a few seconds ago that people talk and it's hardly possible to stop them. In such a case, how do you respond to negative comments coming from others with or without an intention to make you feel miserable about yourself?

For instance, when Candace wore a new bold pink dress to office, her colleague Syrah said, "Yikes! That's way too bright Candace." With her nose up in the air, Syrah ranted on, "I would never wear something like that." What do you think Candace would have said?

"Eh... Yea... I did think it was too bright. Maybe I shouldn't have worn it. Why did I even buy it?"

But Candace did not curse herself. In fact, this is what she said, and please note, with a twinkle in her eyes:

"I know Syrah, this color is really bold. But you know what; it makes me feel bright and happy. Maybe I could spread some of my vivacity to others around me. What say you?"

You bet Syrah was quite taken. And you know what, a couple of weeks later, she might have bought herself a dress the same color!

Candace didn't stop wearing bright-colored clothes. She could carry them off and was comfortable in depicting a vibrant personality. She believed in what she did.

Doesn't this incident agree with the fact – No one can make you feel inferior without your consent?

It's not what people say to you that affects your confidence. It's what you say to yourself after they've stopped talking that either makes or breaks your self-esteem.

Every feeling tells you something, but you should learn to take them with a pinch of salt.

Remember it has been made up by what you have been thinking and saying to yourself.

It will take time to learn them all, but build up gradually and you will start to build up your confidence.

Here are a few feelings and thoughts that you are sure to face sometime or the other. Check what kind of action you can practice in such a case.

FEELING: "I don't feel confident about the way I look"
ACTION: Improve your overall appearance. Would losing or putting on (in case you are painfully thin) some weight make you feel great? If so DO IT! What clothes would your Confidence Role Model wear to feel good? Get a new haircut and treat yourself to some new clothes – it always makes you feel better and more

confident. Buy something new each month and when you put it on, view it as your own confidence booster.

FEELING: "I'm afraid of that person – I'm never confident around her"
ACTION: Just remember, they eat, sleep, go to the toilet just like you do and mostly they have the same problems as you - they just don't show it! Think – How would your Confidence Role Model deal with this person? What would they do?
Remember that confidence is about acting – they are just better actors than you right now. Think of the things you can do that they can't do – how would they feel if the roles were reversed? Getting any closer?

FEELING: "I'm afraid of the feedback and reaction I'm going to get when I complete this piece of work"

ACTION: Hey, as long as you've done everything to the best of your ability, you don't have to worry. And if you do make a mistake or two, what the heck?! Just learn from them for next time. A person who never makes mistakes is not doing anything. Those people who moan and groan about things always seem to do nothing. There are no failures in life as long as you learn from the outcome. You're a winner!

FEELING: "I'm really worried about this…"
ACTION: Time to usher in your Confidence Role Model again (when did you ever let her go, right?). Would my Confidence Role Model worry about this? How would they deal with this situation? What would they do? In the grand scheme of things what will worrying do to this problem? Is there any action I can take to fix this right now?

FEELING: "My friends are really negative thinkers and this just festers onto me when I'm with them"
ACTION: Don't get rid of your friends but make sure you surround yourself with positive and progressive people also. Surround yourself with people who are like your role model.

You know what your friends are like beforehand, so just accept them for what they are. If they are true friends just acknowledge that they are who they are and you are who you are.

FEELING: "I can't do this"
ACTION: Oh yes you can! Break the problem down into small chunks and attack each chunk separately. Nothing is ever as daunting as it first seems. How would your Confidence Role Model do this? Think of a time where you have done something really difficult – think this through in your mind and play it over and over like a video recording before you do the task in hand.

FEELING: "I've never got enough money to do the things that I want"
ACTION: Ask yourself what you are doing about it? Do you have the "more month left at the end of the money" rather than "more money left at the end of the month" problem? Do you plan your budget? Do you know where all your money goes? If you answered yes to the first question and no to the next two, it's time you made a plan of action. For all you know, you may need another career to achieve the lifestyle you want?

FEELING: "I don't feel worthwhile as a person"
ACTION: Put down your strengths on a piece of paper. Don't forget to list down all your achievements in life from your exams, to when you passed your driving test, to the job interviews you cleared etc. Remind yourself that you've already had loads of successes and don't feel so sorry for yourself. After all, no matter where you are in life, there is always someone who is worse off than you. Put things into perspective; ask yourself what your Role Model would do.

More Actions

We are not done yet, so pick up a fresh piece of paper.

Write down all of those confidence destroying statements that you say to yourself or others say to you.

Now, write down what you are going to replace these thoughts with after the statements are made.

Write down next to each statement, why it is downright twaddle.

Confidence sapping friends & colleagues

The people whom you hang out with, that is, family, friends or colleagues, they will have either a positive or negative affect on your levels of self-esteem and confidence.

You are sure to have been around people who are positive, happy and pleasant.

They are the ones who make you feel a welcome sight any day, who smile sincerely, and who encourage you rather than rain you down with advices.

How do they make you feel?

Their personality rubs on to you too, making you feel positive, happy and pleasant. Such lively people can easily sprinkle zest into a boring atmosphere and can fill a room with constructive energy and upbeat vibes.

You must be familiar with the moaners too.

They are always putting people down, they don't like others being successful, and they are jealous and are negative thinkers. Phew! That's a long list and it sure can go on.

Such people bleed dry your energy, bring down your energy levels and in a way take you a million miles away from the level you really want to be operating on. They try and urge you to join their team – a team of non-achievers.

Family members can be grumblers a lot of times, but you can always choose your friends; you can never choose your family!

So what should you do to make sure that the people you hang out with empower and support what you stand for rather than bring you down all of the time?

1. You have the power to choose who you hang out with. Ideally, you want happy, vibrant and positive people. Say, people who are more like Candace and less like Syrah.

2. If you have good friends who are negative and yet you want to hang around them, make a point of letting them know how you feel - if they are true friends, they will respect you for this. If they are negative from time to time, just acknowledge that this is what they are like and block out the negativity.

3. The same can be applied to family. Your more mature family members have behaviours that have been conditioned for years. Appreciate where they have come from and stated before, select and elicit the information that filters through to your brain.

4. And remember to keep this statement in your minds always – Nothing has meaning in life except the meaning you give it.

How to feel Confident all the time

Self-confidence is essential..

The power of the mind is truly remarkable

How you feel in any given moment is linked to:

- **What you are focusing on**
- **The way you are moving and using your body**
- **The language you are using**

No doubt, your mind controls all three.

The moment you feel lethargic or need an instant confidence/ energy boost just change the way you feel by changing the above 3 points.

1. What you are focusing on.

Stay conscious of what you are focusing on in that particular moment.

Are they negative and lethargic thoughts? Low in confidence? Are they indicating that you would fail? Are you telling yourself that you feel low in energy?

Yes?

What would you have to focus on to feel vibrant and full of energy? What should you focus on to feel confident?

On the other hand, if you are feeling vibrant and energized right now, what are you thinking about?

2. The way you are moving and using your body.

This is also called your physiology.

Emotion is created by motion, and the fewer movements you make the less energy you will have!

Moreover, the type of movements you make either pump you up or make you languid and want to doze off.

Observe your body when you are feeling low in confidence.

Are you sitting down? Is your head up or down? Are your shoulders slouched? Are you walking slowly or quickly? Are your facial muscles moving? What are you doing with your hands?

Write down below all the characteristics of a confident person. Imagine there is a confident person before you now. How would they be moving their body?

It's your turn to feel energized and confident. Ready?

Okay!

Copy the movements that you just wrote down when you are feeling low and, WHOA! You'll become confident!

3. The language you are using.

The words you say to yourself both in your mind and out aloud will have an impact on how you are feeling.

What words do you use to describe negative emotions?

Do you say? :

"I'm feeling tired"
"I'm stupid"
"I'm angry"
"I'm livid"
"I'm overwhelmed"
"I'm depressed"

Write down some more common phrases like those above that you use:

The intensity of those negative sayings will have an effect on how you feel and whether you feel confident or not.

What if instead of – **"I'm really nervous"**, you said to yourself – **"I'm really excited"**?

Would it make you feel better?

Of course it would.

The feelings and emotions linked to nervousness and excitement are actually the same. It's just that you are giving the adrenaline right direction.

So, what other words could you replace the negative sayings with?

Try swapping:

"I'm feeling tired" to **"I'm feeling resourceful"**
"I'm stupid" to **"I'm learning"**
"I'm angry" to **"I'm a little annoyed"**

"I'm livid" to **"I'm a little miffed"**
"I'm overwhelmed" to **"I'm feeling busy"**
"I'm feeling insecure" to **"I'm questioning"**
"I'm depressed" to **"I'm not on top of things"**

As the intensity of the words lower, the intensity of the feelings lessen too.

Let's move on with some simple exercises.

Write down 5 old negative sayings or phrases that you say on a consistent basis and replace them with new empowering and less intensified ones:

OLD NEGATIVE PHRASES

1.

2.

3.

4.

5.

NEW EMPOWERING/LOW INTENSITY PHRASES

1.

2.

3.

4.

5.

Just as you lower the intensity of words to lessen negative feelings, you can apply the reverse to feel magnificent and confident every single day!

Change your vocabulary to improve the quality of your day.

How?

Increase the intensity; increase the feeling when you use positive/good words.

Want an example? Here you go…

Instead of saying **"I feel good,"** say **"I feel fantastic!"**

It's as simple as that.

Here are some more:

Change:

"I feel ok" to **"I feel awesome"**
"I feel motivated" to **"I am driven"**
"I feel confident" to **"I feel unstoppable"**
"I feel energized" to **"I feel juiced"**

Change the "good" words of the present to "magnificent" words of the future.

When you implement this, the impact will be AWESOME!

OLD "GOOD" PHRASES

1.

2.

3.

4.

5.

NEW "MAGNIFICENT" PHRASES

1.

2.

3.

4.

5.

Life

How to lead a Confident Life

Congratulations!

You have done a great job on pushing through your Confidence training!

We hope by now you are more of a DOER than just a READER.

With these pages you will get going only if you put into action all that you picked up. Reading alone will be of no good.

Your confidence will shoot high only if you are a doer, and on that note let's kick off the last session.

****
The New Confident You!
****

Are you all pumped up with confidence as you reach the final stages of this book?

Have you been putting into action all those recommendations that you came across in this book?

If yes, we are glad that you are really serious about making a difference in your life by increasing your confidence levels and self-esteem. **Good Going!**

Trust that you are prepared to do an analysis of how you felt before and how you feel now.

Compare by writing them down as this will help you clarify everything and make them official.

We understand this could be difficult, arranging the thoughts without being subjective. But we bet you will feel great once you are done. At least, relieved!

And you know what? If you have done this smoothly, you are already a champion.

Yes! You heard it right! CHAMPION! And you now have that self-confidence you always wanted.

You have taken the first step and you deserve to treat yourself. Go out and watch a movie, or dine in a posh restaurant, or get yourself a new dress.

While you treat yourself, don't forget to take note of how your confidence has been building over the past couple of weeks.

Jot down all the things you have noticed that illustrate that your confidence is improving, no matter how small or large they are.

We will now give you an **8-point reminder** that will perform as a quick reference on how to get confidence in any given situation.

1. **Think through your desired outcome - Ask yourself – "How would a person with confidence do this?"**
2. **Visualize yourself doing the tasks. Close your eyes and see yourself doing it successfully.**

3. **Prepare thoroughly. What are you going to say? How are you going to say it?**
4. **Before you do it, go through it in your mind several times and be positive.**
5. **Put it into perspective - No matter what it is, in 50 years' time will people really care about it?**
6. **DO IT!**
7. **Learn from the outcome you get for next time.**
8. **REWARD yourself for DOING rather than TALKING about doing it!**

****

Well, here you are, all confident and ready to face the world. Hope you have gained enough from this training to last you a lifetime because remember, you only live once and hence you have to make the most of every opportunity and every moment that comes your way.

****

Discover What Your Life is Really About

Life is so short that you cannot wait for your wishes to be fulfilled. Neither is it generous enough to take everything for granted. However, it is possible to design your life any way you can, go out and grab whatever you want said, Charlotte Howard.

Welcome to "How to Get What You Want!"

First of all, you need to have a clear picture of where you are at right now. Then realize what it is that you truly want from life. Develop a clear understanding of what you need and what you do not. The next couple of pages will help you comprehend your wants, and find the ways to make sure that you are going to fulfill them all.

Every woman wants is evaluated on the basis of her successes. However, success does not mean the same thing to everyone. In the first chapter, you will have a close look at what success actually means to you and then we will discuss what the purpose of your life is.

This section is the underpinning on which others are based. Moreover, it deals with the things that set the foundation on what your life is based on.

<u>What is Success?</u>

Every woman wants to be a success in her life. People consider material success as the key to more money, happiness, fulfillment and rewards. Regardless of how differently people perceive it, everyone wants it.

Different people define success differently. And they tend to change their definition with changing times and circumstances as well. For some people, conventional success is more important and it seldom goes beyond money, cars or big homes.

You must have your own definition for success. You can change your definition of success and put it closer to reality. Before that you need to comprehend what success actually means to you.

Write your definition of what success is in the space below or on a piece of paper.

Do not carry on reading this until you have done so.

It may take a good amount of time to sort out your priorities when you define what success means. Don't worry, take your time. If you haven't filled in the above space yet do it now! Don't cheat yourself!

Who is successful?

Mary Jane is a 28-year old single woman. Her job as a Financial Analyst enables her to maintain a posh apartment in the City and own a Lexus. She could afford a vacation anywhere in the world, though she rarely goes out of the City if it's not on an official trip.

Her hectic workload seldom allows Mary Jane to reach home before 7 pm or to go out for a party. Lack of socialization often gives her a feeling of loneliness, though she believes that the money makes up for it. She is ready to put aside her personal feelings for a career that gives her enough money and social status.

A person defines success on the basis of a number of factors. And you are no exception.

Your definition of success is formed by:

- Your upbringing
  Everyone perceives things on the basis of the values he or she has learned in the childhood.

- Your beliefs
  Beliefs, deep-rooted in your mind, affect the way you perceive things.

- Trait
  A particular characteristic that distinguishes you or that is genetically determined may influence the way you perceive things.

- Your attitude

Everyone has an opinion or general feeling about everything.

- Your peers
  You family, friends, colleagues or whoever you maintain a constant contact with can influence the way you perceive things.

- Society
  It is an important factor that has more influence than many of the rest.

- Every experience that you have in life
  Small or big, each and every experience in your life influences the way you perceive things.

All the factors mentioned above, more or less, contribute to what success means to you.

There is a myth that states that people are born winners or born losers.

Nothing could be further from the truth. Nobody is born just to win or lose. The way you live your life makes you a winner or loser.

Even a single sensible timely step can change the entire scenario of your life. You need to sense what the situation demands and act accordingly.

Nothing is worse than looking back after some years and saying "I wish I had done this."

Know where you are going in life

Setting goals is something everybody does regularly. However, few find it in them to go through the plans they set. You need to know where you are going and constantly check and make sure that you are moving in the proper direction.

Creating a vision and a mission statement of what you want out of life will provide you with some direction and momentum to move forward. It can act as a catalyst in accomplishing your task.

What is your life all about?

Different people look at life in entirely different ways. While some people let things happen to them, others go out and make things happen. It's very important to have an understanding of which group you belong to.

If you are driven by a compelling vision, you have a greater chance to feel good about yourself.

If you have a true mission, you have a better chance to know where you are going in your life.

When you feel you are in control of your life and events, you will naturally feel more confident and motivated as a woman to achieve more.

Ask yourself the following question:

What do you really want to get out of life?

A clear vision and a well-defined mission will help you realize the real purpose of your life. Both your vision and mission should express your purpose for existence.

Following is a series of questions for you to ask yourself in order to do some soul searching and to give yourself some insights into what you are all about and why you are here:

- "When I grow up, I want to be a pilot." As a child, what did you dream of becoming?
- Which three people do you think have influenced your life the most and why?
- If you could choose your career and get paid whatever you wanted, what would you opt for?
- What are your top three achievements in life so far? What was so special about them?
- Doing what makes you the happiest in life?
- Who are the three people who you admire the most? What are their characteristics and qualities you admire so much?
- Have you ever helped someone less fortunate than you? If yes, what did you do? If no, why not?
- List out your greatest strengths?
- What steps should you take in life to maximize your strengths?
- What is that one thing for which you would be willing to put everything on the block for? Why?
- Imagine that all the time you spent till now comes back to you. How would you utilize it now? What would you do with the time this second time round?
- There are sure to be results/ events in your life you are happy about? What are these? Which are the results/ events you are unhappy about?
- Is there a word of advice you have picked up from your life so far that you want to pass on to the world?

- Name one thing you value the most in life?
- What would you really like to do with your life?

Answering the questions given above will give you a clear idea about yourself.

The whole point of getting you to think about those questions was to really get you to think about what you want and wanted for your life.

It would be easier for you, after answering the questions, to realize what you want from life and how you are going to get it. If you have answered all the questions given above, write down your own mission statement in the box below:

A mission statement is not a 'to do list.' So it is not easy to write one and it shouldn't be something that is rushed.

Take your time, go for a walk, or take a short break. It's better to get away from the routine environment. Remember, your mission in life is far too important to be skimmed over.

A mission statement needs to be honest. Make sure you actually believe in your mission statement. If you don't, it's a lie. Don't cheat yourself.

Women who do not have an authentic mission in life tend to just have materialistic goals. The greatest problem with such women is they don't know what fulfillment is. After they have achieved, achieved and achieved, they say to themselves "Is that all there is?"

Without a sense of fulfillment, there is no joy.

Mapping Out What You Want in Your Life

Welcome to this section of How to Get What You Want.

The first part was meant to give you an idea about what success is and the emptiness of success without fulfillment.

Hopefully you have put some things into perspective in your life, right?

So, now you have a clear vision and an honest mission statement for your life. The roadmap to a successful and fulfilled life is within your hands. After completing those exercises did you find that you would need to start work on some things and to stop certain things as well?

Assignment 1

Before we carry on, please have a quick read over what you put down in the last section of training. Keeping what you have learned in mind, answer the questions given below:

- What are you going to start to do?
- What are you going to stop?
- What have you been putting up with in the past that you shouldn't have been?
- What are you going to do instead of this?
- What are you going to move towards in the future?
- What was the one learning point that came out of the exercise more than any other?

Anyone can make a new start any time.

Complete the following goal setting section to focus on what you want in the future. To accomplish great things, we must learn to dream first.

You need to dream to make them come true. So, throughout the exercise, keep dreaming. Let there be no limits!

OK, here comes the exercise!

Create Your Goals

Certainty and uncertainty are two phases of life. Both contribute immensely to your confidence and lack of confidence.

In order to feel confident you need to have some certainty in your life. You need to be convinced that what you are doing is contributing to an end result.

People often set goals with the intention of achieving them. Many strive for it, but only a few succeed. A wrong step or small mistake could spoil the efforts of a very long time. Then you will start wondering why, despite all your efforts, success evades you. Such feelings might seriously affect your confidence.

We are all goal seeking women and you are no exception. In fact we set numerous goals a day and strive for them simultaneously in the different areas of our life.

Have you got any goals mapped out for each area of your life?

If not, then read on and complete this exercise.

Goal Creation Exercise:

With regards to the following areas in your life:

- Career
- Relationships
- Fun
- Achievements
- Money

- Possessions

Take 6 pieces of paper for the 6 areas given above. Under each heading, brainstorm for 3 minutes and write down all of the things you would like to achieve in each area.

You don't have to be scared of or worry about the size of your goal. Just get them down and don't think too much about them - Just keep writing!

After you have completed the first part of the exercise you should have 6 pieces of paper full of everything that you would like to achieve for each area.

Next, write down a time limit next to each of the goals. The time limit should be reasonable as well as realistic.

The suggested timescales are:

- Less than 1 year
- 1 – 3 years
- 3 years plus

So, you have got 6 lists of things that you want to achieve in the 6 areas of your life, and the timescale for each.

Next, take your LESS THAN 1 YEAR goals for each area and select the top 2 from each.

So now you have got 12 goals that you can achieve within 1 year.

A strong need or a real motivation is essential to achieve any goal. It is the key. So, before we start to write down an action plan (that's the next chapter) of how to achieve each goal, write down the compelling reasons why achieving each goal is an absolute must for you.

Knowing is as important as doing. You need to check that if your motivations are strong enough to take you to the end.

Unless you have compelling reasons why you MUST make these goals happen, you will not have the motivation to achieve them.

Having goals that are "SHOULDS" will not get you out of bed each day and keep you up late! Moreover too many "SHOULDS" can act as a problem. So, you've got to turn your "I SHOULD DO THIS" to "I MUST DO THIS."

Answer the following questions for each of your goals.

What pleasure will it give you?

What will you be able to do with it?

What will you miss if you don't complete it?

Why is it so important to you?

Why is it a MUST rather than a SHOULD?

To recap then!

- Brainstorm what you want in each area of your life
- Put timescales next to each
- Select your less than 1 year goals
- Pick 2 goals from each
- Write down the compelling reasons why achieving each in less than one year is a must

That's it for now.

In the next section we will have a detailed look at your goals and prepare action plans for each!

Fire The Gun! – How to Take Action

Welcome back, we are very excited to help you improve your life with confidence!

First of all, let's have a quick recap of what we have covered so far.

In the first section you had a look at what success means to you and had written out what you would like to be remembered for long after you have gone.

In the second section you made a list of goals you want to achieve and found out the compelling reasons of why you want to achieve them. Also, you had set time limits for each goal to be achieved.

OK, now take the list of goals out, and re-read the reasons. Do they make you feel energized and motivated, and induce a feeling of necessity inside you? Do you feel achieving them is something you can't afford missing?

If they don't, you need to find out better reasons. It does not deserve a place in your list otherwise. Scrap the goal altogether!

You will only achieve a goal when it becomes an absolute MUST for you to do so. A goal is nothing but a daydream if you don't have compelling reasons behind it.

It's not the goal but the reasons behind it that make you take action.

Following are some goals you might have included in your list:

Losing some weight
Running your own business
Working harder
Spending more time with your family
Being more assertive

Teaching your child to ride a bicycle
Gaining a better job or promotion
Doing charity work
Owning a new car
Improving your relationship with your boss
Writing a diary
Earning more money
Learning to swim
Controlling your temper
Paying more attention to your clothes

The following is a simple description about setting and achieving a goal.

First of all, you must decide what your GOAL actually is. Then you must define it comprehensively. Next you can lay out the steps by which you intend to reach the goal. And finally you must put a deadline or a time limit to achieve your goal.

And, needless to say, you must also have a genuine reason why you want to achieve the goal.

The goal setting process can be compared with a long distance car journey.

You wouldn't think of planning the journey without knowing where you were going to go and why you want to go there.

You would have mapped out the route, and have an idea of the time it would take to reach your destination

Sounds familiar, doesn't it?

Well, goal setting uses exactly the same method, except in this case, you are the car and the journey is your life.

When it comes to setting your goals, clarity and preciseness are most required qualities. Generalizations and vague ideas won't get you anywhere.

Ask any woman on the street to define their goals in life. You would invariably get responses such as "I want to be rich," "I want to be happy" or "I want to be famous."

Never let yourself be fooled into thinking that these were goals. They are not.

They are just generalizations that are desired by every woman.

A goal needs to be defined in detail. Or a true goal is something you can define in detail. This step comes just after the identification of the goal. If, for example, one of your goals is to buy a new car, you must define the model, the color, the interior, the price and other details.

Always make sure that you can picture it clearly in your mind and try to get away from generalizations.

Be specific and be precise.

GOAL - TO BUY A NEW CAR

Details
MODEL - BMW 3 series sports convertible
COLOUR - Metallic Blue
INTERIOR - Beige Leather
PRICE - $35,450
EXTRAS - Air Conditioning, CD player, Electric Windows..........

Given above are the primary details. You can go to secondary or tertiary details to exactly know what you want.

Consider the following questions:

What color are the seats?

What brand is the CD player?

Has it got Electric Windows?

Does it have a sunroof?

Is the sunroof electric?

Has it got alloy wheels?

HOW TO ACHIEVE YOUR GOAL - PLANNING AND ACTION

Now you know what you want to achieve and you have defined it in detail. The next step is to actually plan and map out exactly how you are going to achieve it.

Your desire is not enough to achieve a goal. You need to have the courage, will and an action plan to achieve a goal.

Remember, it is a lot easier to achieve a goal if it is broken down into a series of sub-goals. Each sub-goal, with its own specific deadline, should lead you to the ultimate one. Moreover, when a goal breaks into many sub-goals, you are expected to tackle it sequentially, completing one sub-goal before moving to next.

Consider the following example.

You want to lose some weight. Make the goal more specific.

So the redefined goal is to lose 12 lbs in 8 weeks.

The next step would be the breaking down of the large goal into sub-goals. You could set yourself sub-goals of losing 1.5 lbs per week for the 8 weeks.

Make a table and post it on a wall so that you can see it. Suppose you weigh 12 pounds over weight now and want to lose the 12 lbs, your chart would look something like the one below:

GOAL: TO LOSE SOME WEIGHT

SPECIFICS: 12 lbs in 8 Weeks
WEIGHT AS AT xx/xx/06 = 12 lbs over
TARGET WEIGHT AS AT xx/xx/

	GOAL - LOSS	WEIGHT	ACTUAL
End of week 1	1.5 lbs	<u>145</u>	
End of week 2	1.5 lbs	<u>143.5</u>	
End of week 3	1.5 lbs	<u>142</u>	
End of week 4	1.5 lbs	140.5	
End of week 5	1.5 lbs	139	
End of week 6	1.5 lbs	137.5	
End of week 7	1.5 lbs	136	
End of week 8	1.5 lbs	134.5	

Losing 1.5 lbs a week does not look like a big deal, right?

Action Plan

What you have prepared is nothing but a well-defined, systematically divided goal. Now you need an action plan to achieve the goal. So, devise an exercise plan and a healthy diet to help you achieve your goal.

Brainstorm all of the actions you need to do in order to achieve this goal and chunk them into activities of similar nature.

For example:

Exercise – What exercises? How often? Do I need new kit? How much?
Diet – What food? How often? How many calories? Shopping List?
Type of gym – Locations? Prices? Clients?

You can also plan what exercise you are going to do on a particular day and how much time you are going to spend. Make another table, similar to the one you have already prepared, for your exercise routine and healthy eating plan. And always try to stick closely to the schedule.

The method used to illustrate the weight-loss example is often referred to as stair-stepping or chunking, which means breaking a big goal down into smaller components. I give thanks to my mentor Ann Sieg for teaching me more about chunking. By doing this, beside many other advantages, you can enjoy any number of successes even before achieving your final goal.

The stair-stepping method is similar to eating a Pizza!

**Try to eat an entire pizza in one mouthful….no you can't.
By cutting it into smaller, bite-sized pieces you can make it more eatable and more enjoyable.**

Break your goals down and they will become a lot easier for you to achieve. By focusing your attention on the comparatively easier sub-goals, you can make great progress towards your final goal without feeling overwhelmed.

If you concentrate on your sub-goals, your major goal will take care of itself.

GET THE TIMING RIGHT!

Setting reasonable and realistic deadlines for each sub-goals as well as the final goal is very important. Putting things off until tomorrow or next week will turn into another tomorrow or another week.

Let's take a look at a word no aspiring successful woman should have in her vocabulary. Meet **PROCRASTINATION!**

See how many ways it can affect your pursuit of success.

You could put things off by *never choosing to do anything.*

You could put things off by choosing to do something, *but you never start doing it.*

You could put things off by starting something, *but you never continue doing it.*

And then you could continue doing something, *but you never finish it.*

At every stage of your action plan you must set yourself deadlines so that you don't put things off until tomorrow.

Do Not Procrastinate

Breakdown your goal into a number of sub-goals
☐
Allot your time for each sub-goal
☐
Formulate deadlines to achieve each sub-goal and as well as the ultimate one
☐
Be honest in respecting your deadlines

This can be called the TIMETABLE TO SUCCESS.

Setting achievable and realistic goals and deadlines is very important. For example, one cannot expect to pass her driving test after only 2 lessons. Passing after 20 lessons is more attainable and realistic.

Never set a goal that exceeds your ability. However, at the same time, you need to ensure the maximum exploitation of the time allotted. The gap between potential and performance must be the minimum.

Success breeds success.

Setting realistic goals can help create the habit of achieving them. This will build up your confidence and help you attain more demanding goals. Moreover, by setting goals that are measurable and achievable, you can easily make corrections to them if you go off target.

If you are a manager or have people working for you, please bear the following in mind.

Setting unattainable targets or making unrealistic demands will only do harm to the motivation, self-esteem and confidence of your workforce and will result in a reduction in productivity.

If you ask too much of yourself, the same will happen to you as well. You will become de-motivated and will lose interest in doing it.

The most successful women in the world are those who can identify their own abilities and limitations. And the best managers are those who can identify their employees' abilities and limitations and then set work/goals that will stretch their abilities without exceeding the limit. Such managers invariably have highly motivated employees. Their approach makes the subordinates feeling worthwhile and encourages them to push the limits.

There is a fine line that divides goals that are too easy to achieve and goals that are probably out of reach. You can distinguish them by using your common sense, knowing your strengths and weaknesses, knowing your potential to develop and learn, and by using trail and error method.

You need to set specific goals for different areas of your life. You can set a goal that will help you take a leap in your career, or you can set a goal that will gain you personal rewards. Create specific Action Plans and apply appropriate techniques in each case.

Following are some techniques and tips that you can use in setting goals and attaining them.

There is a saying, "A verbal contract isn't worth the paper it is written on."

It is of no good saying that you have got a goal if you haven't written it down. What you need is self-commitment, and writing things down is a start to developing it.

Setting Goals

An Example:

What?

Lose 10 lbs in weight

Why?

It will give me greater confidence, enhance my self esteem, and will make me more attractive to men

How?

Exercise, Diet, Allocating Time, Gym or home, etc

Chunking

- Finding Gym, exercise routines, kit, frequency
- Nutrition
- Time Management and organization

Sub-goals

- Lose 2 lbs per month
- Buy 1 new item of clothing each month
- Visit gym 4 times per week
- Increase distance or resistance each time

Timelines

Major Goal attained within 5 months xx/xx/2008
X weight in 2 months yy/yy/2008

Review
What's going well? What are the results? Do I need to adjust?

Adjust
Make sure that you write everything down.

If you haven't already started formulating your goals, the following exercises will be helpful.

For each of your goals brainstorm and write down whatever you will need to achieve.

What will you need?
Are you experienced enough?
Who can help?
What will you have to do?
Is there a cost?
Do you need any equipment?
Do you require any capital?

Chunk all of the actions into 3 or 4 main areas and then class these as sub-goals. Give deadlines for each.

Then, GO FOR IT!

Achieving these goals will give you great self-confidence. It will also put you in the right frame of mind to achieve greater feats.

Other uses of goal attainment

The use of goal attainment should be a part of your daily routine.

If you are attending a course at work, determine what exactly you want to get out of it and why i.e. realize your goals and objectives.

If you have got an important interview, set yourself the goal of getting up an hour earlier to the usual time so that you can go through your notes once again.

Setting well-defined goals and achieving them in a systematic manner will increase your confidence and efficiency.

If you have staff to manage, give them realistic as well as demanding targets. No matter what their experience or expertise, you will get the best out of them. It will also help them improve their skills and productivity.

Think over the various points discussed in today's session. Go through your assignments again.

Overcoming Problems and Difficulties

The way to success is no bed of roses. Whilst trying to attain your goals, there will be many obstacles in your way. You might face both physical and mental difficulties.

Instead of beating yourself up or giving in, you need to learn from setbacks. As you know, a diamond cannot be polished without friction.

Use obstacles and failures as an opportunity to polish your skills. You will have to sail with the wind sometimes, and sometimes against it. But, you must sail, and not drift nor lie at anchor.

So, what matters is your attitude. This section we will have a look at your beliefs and let you know if you have got the attitude to thrive under pressure and to succeed.

Refocusing after setbacks

How many times have you started a diet, stopped exercising, or tried something new and went back to where you were when a setback or obstacle occurred. Women often stumble over obstacles and even consider them as excuses for their failures.

Setbacks and difficulties are inevitable in life. They often challenge your skills and temper.

There are two ways to face difficulties.

- ♦ You can either change the difficulty or change yourself to be able to deal with it.
- ♦ You can deal with difficulties properly and make use of the experience to enhance your confidence or you can deal with them incorrectly and let them seriously damage your confidence.

If you can see and face challenges in a positive way, you will gain immense experience and knowledge from it.

Your response to issues and difficulties

Failure should never be considered as a source of discouragement, but a motivation. You know how Helen Keller, a mute and blind woman, went on to become a world-famous speaker and author. Your ability to deal with challenges can be converted into a virtue by asking positive empowering questions yourself.

There is an unwritten rule that says:
Ask your mind a stupid question and you will get a stupid answer!

So, if, after a setback, you ask yourself something like

"Why does this always happen to me, I never have any luck?"

Your mind will probably come out with:

"Because you are useless and good things do not happen to you!"

Instead, if you ask yourself a positive empowering question like:

"What did I learn from this setback for next time?"

Your mind will switch into solution mode and come out with some excellent tips.

Following are some points to ponder about when setbacks do occur:

- Be brave enough to acknowledge what has happened. Don't hide away from it. These things happen. So what?

- Ask yourself as many positive empowering questions as you can.

For example:
What is good about this situation?
How can I make the most of this situation?
What can I learn from it?
What are the facts about this problem?
How can we make it a success next time?

- Acknowledge the fact that setbacks occur to everyone and you are not being singled out.

- View setbacks as a challenge to overcome rather than an issue or problem.

Get your belief system right for success!

It is difficult to get away from discouraging thoughts after a failure. Make a list of the negative thoughts and questions that usually come into your mind after a setback. Also think about the equally discouraging answers you normally have.

Then make a list of some encouraging questions you can ask instead. Obviously you also have some encouraging answers. Try to ask these encouraging questions every time you face a difficulty. Making it a habit can basically change your attitude to adversities.

How to Develop Strong Inner Beliefs

Development of a strong inner belief system is essential to avoid discouraging thoughts. You can clarify yourself by asking some self-assuring questions. Such clarifications will lead to self-acceptance, which, in turn, will give you the much needed energy and room to grow. Remember, He who conquers himself conquers the world.

Self-acceptance is all about how much one values, loves, and accepts herself, rather than how much she feels valued, loved, or accepted by others. Having a strong value/inner belief system is very much dependent on your ability to accept yourself. So you need to accept your identity, your feelings and your outlook of the world.

The ability to appreciate one's own worth is a great virtue. People with healthy self-esteem are able to feel good about themselves and take pride in their skills and accomplishments.

People who consider themselves as having no admirable qualities may develop a low self-esteem. They may feel as if no one likes them or accepts them or they can't do well in anything. The problem becomes worse when someone whose acceptance is important constantly puts him/her down.

The benefits of a strong inner belief system are many;

- Stronger self-confidence
- Healthy self-esteem
- Greater life satisfaction
- Comfort with self and others

But how exactly does one go about developing a strong inner belief system?

Consider the following questions.

Finding answers to these can help you distinguish yourself in the group.

1. **Explore what you currently believe about work, life, people, and yourself.**

   You can try a free-writing exercise. Write each word (work, life, etc.) at the top of a page (one for each page) and then a free associate for each word. Write down whatever thoughts might be conjured up by the word at the top of the page.

   Write until each page is full.

2. **How much of what you believe is your own?**

   Take a look at what you wrote on each page.

   Identify messages that may have come from parents, friends, family, peers, teachers, etc. You can see that some thoughts appear under almost every section. Identify the recurring themes.

   Now, highlight the things that truly reflect who you are and what you believe.

3. **How much of it is enabling and how much disabling?**

   The messages of others can be encouraging or discouraging.

   Now, look at the messages and thoughts that reflect your own inner belief system. How do they make you feel, empowering or limiting?

4. **What do you want to believe?**

   Consider your true beliefs, the thoughts and messages you firmly believe in.

Do they reflect how you want to feel about life, work, people, and yourself?

Take a blank paper and write down each idea or thought that are considered right by others on the left hand. On the right hand side write down your alternative; how you'd like to feel/think about each.

Reprogram yourself by identifying these limiting thoughts as they pop into your head, and replacing them with the thoughts and ideas you identified on the right hand side of the paper.

Continue this exercise, and you will find the old limiting thoughts creeping up less and less and the new empowering thoughts substituting them.

5. **What messages about life, people, work, and yourself did you get from family as you shaped your personality?**

    Family, your primary social unit, can influence you more than most other institutions.

    Family members have the tendency to repeat their messages. If you have chosen to reprogram any of their thoughts, values or beliefs, then be prepared to counter these beliefs whenever a family member articulates them.

6. **What's your response when you express your belief and someone disagrees?**

    There can be many who do not agree with your beliefs and ideas. Consider how you might respond, should you share your beliefs with others and find that they disagree.

    You don't have to change your mind.

> There is nothing wrong in someone else believing differently from your beliefs. People are different and that's what makes the world go round after all.
>
> Simply convey that you see life/work/people/etc. differently, and then reconfirm your belief by repeating it to yourself.

As you explore your answers to these questions and the exercises associated with each, you'll begin to realize the strength of your inner belief system.

It is like the spirit that gives you life. You don't have to always experience or express its presence. It remains within you as long as you live.

Expression of an idea is a difficult job. You need a great amount of confidence to express your beliefs in an unwavering fashion. People will challenge you and come forward with counterarguments.

Consider it as an opportunity to test your ability to continue with your belief system intact as part of you own personal growth.

Once your belief system has been strengthened, you will find that others, having less confidence in their own beliefs, will seek you out. Also, never remain stagnant. You need to grow by helping and encouraging others to tap into their own belief system and follow the process you used.

That's it for this chapter.

How to Keep Motivated and Make the Changes

After serious contemplation, the goals have been written down, broken into sub goals, actions plans have been charted, and you have started implementing the steps you have carefully planned…however…but….still…yet…there are those mixed feelings, distractions, or some stumbling blocks you are facing that's casting doubts…should I go on….is something wrong…

Here's Carol's experience along the lines given above, something you might easily correlate with. What did she do?

Carol Jenkins had enrolled for a German course. The objective behind doing that was simple. She was working at a firm, which had its corporate office in Germany. Employees with fluency in German get a chance to work at the corporate office for 6 months to one 1 year. An opportunity, if used properly could result in a promotion.

The language course was of 6 months duration, and it involved giving up on some precious weekend time both for classes and coping up with assignments. And, Carol was a very popular girl.

In the first month, everything went okay. But in the second month, those invitations she had been rejecting looked more and more appealing. In the third month, the German course became a royal pain. She was also not doing well in her classes.

Finally, her friend who had been silently observing her distress pointed out, "Do you really want the certification or not? If not, forget it. Better to waste three months than 6 months."

Carol's obvious response was, "You do not understand………….."

"Well, I might not but in the last month, you have been taking out your frustration on everyone around you. Your classes are also suffering. It's either letting go three months more of weekend fun or the German course. At this rate, I do not see you getting the certification. It requires an honest effort to study languages if nothing else," her friend replied.

It was decision time for Carol, and she understood. She opted for finishing the German course for the chance to work in Germany and the opportunity for promotion looked more attractive.

You need to be as committed and as motivated to work on them on the 5th, 6th, or 10th week as you were in the 1st.

There are all the probabilities that you might face setbacks.

More powerful setbacks are those mixed feelings and temptations that seems to make you 'take things easy for a while' or procrastinate or simply slow down.

Have a look over the goals that you have written and the reasons why you want to achieve them.

Do they still give a tingle of excitement? Do they still mean a lot to you?

If they do not, then maybe the reasons behind achieving them were not compelling enough.

Check again whether your goals were 'Must Have's or 'Nice to Have's.

A list of MUST HAVE goals will give you the required focus to accomplish them in time. The real reason why people miss goals is because they have NICE HAVES on their lists.

"It would be nice to lose some weight"
"It would be nice to have a new job"

These NICE HAVES are not going to get you up early and keep you up late!

Here is a formula that will help you to change anything you want to and to get you to take action!

It will help you understand the forces at play while you are making a decision on whether changing or doing something is a 'must have' or 'nice to have.'

The Change Formula

There is a simple equation that you can apply to anything and everything while you are making a decision on whether you want to do something or not.

$$D \times V \times P > C$$

Where D stands for Dissatisfaction with the status quo

To make a visible positive change, you must be unhappy with the present situation.

V stands for Vision

This is another basic requirement. You must have a vision of the situation or position you want to achieve. And you must also have an idea of why you want it.

P stands for Practical steps

You must have an action plan of what you need to do. You need to be aware of each and everything you will have to change.

And C stands for Cost of changing

You must have an idea about what the changes will cost you. What will you have to sacrifice? Will you have to change your beliefs?

The **D**, **V** and **P** factors together form your desire to change.

However, the change will occur only if your desire is greater than the associated costs of changing **(C)**.

People welcome making short term sacrifices to achieve a goal. But they tend to give up if it exceeds a limit, when the cost of changing is greater than the desire to change.

You need to identify the potential problems before you start working for a goal, by using methods like the Change formula.

Moreover, an unachieved goal could be another blow to your self-esteem. So, it's important to be well aware of the situation in advance and avoid giving up half way through.

People often comment, "I have no will-power." This probably means that they are enjoying something else and not what they are doing.

If you would be much happier without making the sacrifices, then making them would not be worth it.

Now, once again take a look at the things you have written down. Apply the formula whenever you find it difficult to take a decision.

> **SHOULD I CHANGE?**
> Remember
> $D \times V \times P > C$

How to Live The Life You Want

The most important factor that goes into determining one's success is what goes on in her mind.

Where you are today and what you are today is because of your own mental attitude towards yourself and others. And you alone can change it. All that is needed is a change of your attitude.

The mental attitude that you carry is actually more important than it seems. It could be affecting your life without your knowledge.

Your mental attitude could either take you up the path of success or down the depths of failure.

And changing it is only in your hands.

In this section, we shall see what the correct mental attitude actually is. Chances are that you already have it. But if you haven't, no worries!

You can always acquire it!

We already know how important motivation is and how it can work wonders in one's life. We shall further talk about this activity that gets you off your butt and kick starts you into action.

ATTITUDE - A little thing makes a BIG difference

Whatever you do in life, it is the attitude that you have before, during, and after doing it that determines your success or failure.

Now picture a basketballer taking a penalty shot.
What do you think is going through her mind?

A goal?

Whether the coach will save it?

Or if the ball will end up somewhere off on the court?

There is but a simple rule that you should apply to your thinking in everything you do.

> ***Think Positively and you will get positive results.***
>
> ***Think Negatively and you will get negative results.***

It's as simple as that!

Ok, now that that's clear, complete this exercise.

The exercise will enable you to understand the thoughts of positive and negative people.

Think of the different people you know well – your friends, relatives and colleagues.

Classify all these people under two heads – negative thinkers and positive thinkers. As you know them well, this shouldn't be a very difficult task.

POSITIVE PEOPLE	NEGATIVE PEOPLE

There must be something which made you feel that they are positive-minded or negative-minded. Something that they said, or their reaction to something, etc.

In the box below, write out all those words that describe why you feel that the people under the heading 'positive people' are positive.

What do they say? How do they act? What do they do?

Now prepare another list. Here you have to classify the same people listed before into the two categories – successful and non-successful. Remember, it is your perception of whether they are a success or not.

SUCCESSFUL	NON-SUCCESSFUL

Now look at the two tables you have.

In all probability, you will find that most of the people you categorized as successful people are those who are positive-minded. Similarly, most of the people rated as unsuccessful will belong to the negative thinking lot!

Now you see!

Successful people in life are always positive people

They are the people who

- know what they want
- are optimistic
- expect the best
- expect to win

Negative people in turn, are pessimistic. They look for the worst in everything and expect to fail. These people tend to moan and complain a lot, and always try to put people down.

The way both positive and negative people handle problems is very different.

While positive-minded persons will look for solutions to the problems and a means to proceed further, the negative-minded persons will lose confidence. They will criticize themselves for having chosen that path and will be convinced that he is beaten even before he starts.
Everything that you choose to think, affects your life. The one thing that can bring success or failure in one's life is attitude.

Now think that you are a person who has come to attend an interview at an office.

Picture this.

You are sitting on one of those comfortable chairs outside the interview room in the office, your certificates and papers ready with you.

Now, what exactly is going through your mind as you sit there?

Let's look at it in two ways!
As a **negative-minded person**, you may think along the lines of – what on earth am I doing here? I haven't got any chance of getting this job. Neither do I have the required qualifications nor any

experience. Most probably I will go in there and make a fool of myself in front of everyone. Why did I decide to come here at all?

As a **positive-minded person**, you will be confident and ready to face anything. You will probably think this way. If I have got this far, it is because of my own efforts. So I must be really good. And if I'm good, then I've got a great chance of getting the job. I have got the experience and qualifications and I will say only the right things when questioned. So I'm ready!

The thinking of both the persons is miles apart. The positive-minded person is confident and actually looking forward to attending the interview. In contrast, the negative-minded person is literally on the verge of running away. She doubts herself and dreads the approaching interview. The last thing she has is faith in herself.

Give a thought to this….

Which person do you think stands more of a chance of getting the job?

Put yourself in the shoes of the company boss. Which of the two people would you prefer working for you?

A positive mental attitude obviously boosts one's confidence. It gives the person a power that draws towards them the favorable circumstances, things and people that they think about the most.

Success is something everybody is after. But believe it or not, your attitude may actually be repelling the very thing you are after.

A positive mind attracts opportunities for success while a negative mind fends them off. In fact, a negative-minded person doesn't even take up the opportunities that come along. Why? She is busy focusing on the next time she is going to fail.

A SHORT CASE STUDY – When unemployed

Unemployment. Those who have been through it will know. It's terrible!

Nancy did not have a job. Neither did she have any money. There were numerous jobs that she wasn't even applying for as she was sure that he stood no chance in getting them.

She had the mindset of a loser. She had what we just saw to be a negative mind.

Finally she decided to change herself. She made it a point to think positively in all situations. And what a difference that made! Her life changed!

The glass that was once looked half empty to him now seemed half full.

The results were amazing. Nancy started to radiate confidence and optimism instead of the usual feelings of self-pity and failure. This attracted the right kinds of people to her. With all the pieces of the puzzle put together, success just had to come to her.

So you see the connection?

Positive-thinking □ Success

Suppose you are at a party.

What kind of people would you be drawn towards in a party?

Would it be…..

- a good-humored person who looks at things positively and spreads laughter?

OR

- a miserable looking person who has nothing to talk about but depressing things?

Doesn't require much thinking does it?

Another valuable lesson you could do with is this:

You may find yourself in a difficult situation sometimes, but then don't forget that someone else could be in a much worse situation.

Tammy was the only daughter of her parents. It was Christmas and she expected them to buy a new pair of shoes for her. But her parents could not afford anything at that time. She complained and said such words as "you don't care about me at all" and walked out of the house. Angry as she was, she kicked at everything she saw on the path. Suddenly she stopped in her tracks. She saw before her a woman without any feet! It dawned upon her how lucky she was. "What if I don't have new shoes, am I not lucky to have my two feet?" she told herself. Her parents were glad to find their daughter happy and not complaining anymore when she came back.

Your greatest potential asset is your ability to believe.

The only problem is that you can't benefit from it unless you have what is required- a positive attitude.

You earlier saw that successful people are positive people.

Now ask yourself this-

Am I one of them? Do I think positively?

No matter what mindset you have, there are ways to change it. There are techniques that you could apply to cultivate positive habits in yourself.

You can learn them all....right here!

These techniques have helped people form and keep a positive mental attitude. It has bettered their lives. If it worked for them, why won't it work for you?

Coming up is a bit of practical advice that you could very well act upon. You may be an unemployed woman desperately looking for a job or even the Managing Director of a company. The suggestions are recommended for everyone to apply in their life.

How to Form and Keep a Positive Mental Attitude

To get a positive mental attitude, first of all what you need to do is think and act on the "CAN DO" approach of every activity instead of the "NO CAN'T DO" approach.

Positive people look for answers while negative people look for questions.
There's a poem by Joyce.C. Lock, which has these lines

> If I were a hammer, I'd miss the nail
>
> If I were a knife, I'd cut a finger as well
>
> If I were a letter, I'd be lost in the mail

There are many more such lines in this poem but I can't recollect. Do you also think on such lines? Are you a problem seeker or a solution seeker?

The negative persons are, in short, problem seekers. They believe that problems and obstacles cannot be surpassed. As against that, positive people, no matter what problem they are facing, look for solutions.

All it takes is a smile!

Go back to the lists about positive and negative people that you had created before. Look at the positive people listed on it.

Think it over:

Don't these people smile and laugh a lot more and appear happier than the negative thinkers?

It may seem very silly, but there is a lot of power associated with a smile. A smile is always returned with a smile.

So now onwards, follow this rule - **Smile more often!**

That doesn't mean you have to walk around with a silly grin on your face all the time. Smile when you speak to someone, smile as you walk down the street, smile when looking at yourself in the mirror, smile even when speaking on the phone.

You will be amazed by the good feeling that it generates within you. You feel better and project a positive image to others, which attracts opportunities and more people towards you.

Remember, positive people are happy people and negative people are not.

Happy people seem to be more attractive and pleasant to others compared to gloomy people. Isn't this an added bonus for you?

Pat people on the back

Maria had got a very good position at a local firm. Though the work was something she enjoyed doing, she was never satisfied. Her boss never appreciated her work. She worked very hard and received a lot of appreciation from her colleagues. However her boss merely looks at the work and grumbles. She had been feeling down since she joined till her colleagues confided in her that the man was like that. He never appreciated good work. Instead there was no end to his criticism.

There are many people we see in life who jump at the chance of criticizing a person when something goes wrong. Moreover, these people don't even acknowledge you when you are right!

To create and reflect a positive mental attitude, start complimenting people. If you already have the habit, increase the number of times you do it.

If your partner buys a new piece of clothing and looks attractive, don't just notice that. Tell them so!

You don't lose anything by complimenting someone, do you? And anyway, a compliment never goes waste.

So, compliment your staff and colleagues on their work.

Compliment your child on making it to the football team.

The general idea is that you feel good by making others feel good and it enhances your Positive Mental Attitude. What more, you also enhance the Positive Mental Attitude of the people you compliment!

Merely complimenting people is not enough. The way we treat them is also important. Just follow this simple rule:

Treat others as we would like to be treated ourselves

This involves treating everyone as though they the most important person in the world- because to them it stands true!

The laws of Success state that whatever you hand out in life, you get back at least ten times as much of it.

Connect this rule to life. If you make other people feel worthwhile, useful and valuable, you too are bound to be treated in the same manner- ten times as much.

Research has shown that a customer will tell at least ten people if their expectations from a company have been met with or exceeded, or even if their complaint was dealt with promptly and efficiently.

The same happens if you exceed the expectations of your friends, your boss and your colleagues. You will find yourself becoming popular, highly regarded and noted.

Now comes a warning.

When you compliment people and treat them with respect, be sure that you are doing so genuinely. You must mean what you say.

Believe, conceive and achieve

Start believing that success to you is inevitable.

Whatever task you are given, picture success in your mind. Burn the thought into your subconscious mind. Keep yourself focused on the outcome that you want to achieve in what you do. The mind can achieve anything that it believes and conceives.

You will be surprised to know that there is a giant asleep within yourself. You can direct her to do anything that you want.

You have no idea what you are capable of. Don't underestimate yourself. Believe it, the power of your mind and imagination is truly exceptional.

You can think your way to almost anything in life - success, happiness, illness and even death.

Realize that your mind can't distinguish between thoughts and reality. If you feed it with negative thoughts, your mind will mistake it as something that is actually happening.

Remember those times when you are at home all alone. You seemed to hear every bump, grind and creak clearly, isn't it? Didn't you feel that the clock was ticking very loudly and the tap was dripping like never before?

The same sounds, you would never have heard if you had company!
Why does that happen?

Because your mind is expecting to hear them.

Rehearsal practice- "You've succeeded before you have even begun"

Get yourself introduced to what is called Rehearsal practice. This is an important technique that can enhance your positive mental attitude.

Use the power of your mind to get better results. Put to use that awesome power of imagination that could be now rusting away.

Whatever situation you are put to, rehearse it over once in your mind. Believe it, if you play it over in your mind before you do it better.

By doing so, you are training your subconscious to behave in a certain way to obtain the result that you so much desire.

Let's go back to the job interview.

If you go over in your mind what the interview will probably be like, you can be more prepared. You could imagine things the kind of questions going to be asked, the possible scenario in the interview room, etc. With this done, you will be ready for whatever the interviewer throws at you.
You can use this method in anything that you do. It applies to everything from a driving test to a presentation to hitting a golf

shot. Rehearsal practice is also called visualization. It is another form of focusing on the desired outcome.

Before a presentation you could imagine yourself doing the presentation, tackling the questions that the audience asks. You can have a look at possible questions and be well prepared.

Prior to a speech you could imagine it happening at the venue.

If you have a party at home, let the party happen once in your mind.

In all cases you will realize if you have missed out on anything.

That's visualization! It really helps!

So start today, from right now!

Mentally rehearse or visualize any situation that you find challenging.

Look at athletes on television before a big race or long jump. They will be mentally preparing themselves and going over and over in their mind how they will run or jump. They will be visualizing themselves succeeding.

Apply visualization to the goals in your life. Take 5 minutes of your day for them. Close your eyes and think that you have already achieved the goals. Picture what your life is like, now that you have achieved your goals (in your mind).

You will be fascinated by the end-results.

Now in the midst of all this positive thinking, what if a negative thought creeps in?

Rachel was preparing for a presentation that she was to do before a very important client. Winning the client was very important for her company. All hopes were on her. She was always very confident and that was mainly why she was given the task. The pressure of everybody's expectations was weighing down on her. And yet it didn't seem to affect her. She had thought over the presentation many times in her mind and had won the client.

Once or twice, negative thoughts like "what if I forget what I have to say?"; "what if I'm not able to answer some question the client asks?" seeped in. She brushed them all aside with poise and told herself she had it in her to do well.

What more was needed? She did her best in the presentation and won the client.

So what do you have to do when a negative client finds its way into your mind?

Stop right there, get rid of the negative thought and replace it with a positive thought.

That's easier said than done- you will say.

Ok, try this way. Tell/ask yourself the following every time you experience a negative thought:

"Is this thought really important in the grand scheme of things?"

"What can I change about this thought to make it positive?"

"Think back through past experiences that have been worse and put this thought into the picture"

"Why did that person say what he said? What was behind it? They probably have the problem, not me."

Focus on success and watch, as the people, opportunities and outcomes come your way

Most attributes used to describe a winner are those that can be seen in first class salespeople.

Think of any salesman in any shop or anywhere. If he talks nicely to you and takes care of your requirements, you will say he is nice. Many times you end up buying a product only because of the person.

Salesmanship has got a lot to do with attitude. Whatever we do in life, we are selling ourselves or something, and a person with a negative mindset can sell nothing.

Don't believe it?

What do you think you are doing at an interview, during a presentation, while talking to someone or even when you are on a date?

Yes, you are selling yourself! And that requires you to be positive.

You need a positive attitude to attain your goals. Even for growth, development and progress in life you need a positive mind.

In the journey called life, you have to maintain a positive attitude when faced with opposition from other people or adverse situations.

If you don't have a Positive Mental Attitude, you usually end up being a loser.

If you remain positive and make sure that you are not susceptible to the negative influences of other people- YOU WILL SUCCEED.

Remember this:

All of the world's most successful people have had setbacks in their quest for success.

Your success is not about how many times you fall. It's about how many times you pick yourself after falling. Only persistence can take you to success.

In Summing Up

Without a positive attitude you will find it difficult to achieve anything in life.

Remember, it is your attitude that determines your success.

People who are negative-minded never get anywhere. They are invariably unsuccessful.

Throughout this topic we have seen the advantages of a Positive Mental Attitude. Make sure that you implement these techniques in your life right away!

Think positively and the world is your oyster.

Think negatively and you are doomed to failure.

Any hesitation on what to choose? No way!

MAXIMIZING YOUR POTENTIAL

It is important that you know your goals in life. We have already seen the importance of goal setting and goal attainment. It is vital that you know what you want to do with your life and where you want to go.

You should also know what kind of person you want to be as well.

The way you look, your attire, your possessions, what you say and how you say it, etc – everything goes into determining whether you are successful.

You will be and feel your best when you are winning. So care to look your best too!

Most successful women/winners constantly try to improve areas of their total presentation. They understand and accept that it is a vital factor that helps them maximize their potential.

Now, there is something that you should understand here.

Don't mistake the tendency of these people to change such aspects of their life as something that stems from a feeling of inadequacy or inferiority.

A feeling of inadequacy is by no means the reason for winners and successful women making improvements in their appearance and other areas of their life.

These people are confident about themselves, and know that they are brilliant in their own way. Yet they keep trying to improve even further.

Self Image

You will have a mental perception of how you would like others to see you and what type of a person you would like to be. It is important that you have such a picture of yourself.

The self-image that you show everyone is supposed to be the external result of your internal self-esteem.

You must be meeting plenty of people in your everyday life. Now think over.

How many of them have you seen who walk around with their head bent low and back crouched?

What image do you feel is conveyed about their self-esteem?

Do you think they would be able to sell themselves?

The very impression they project is that of a loser. A person who fears challenges and is not confident about herself.

In contrast, winners present a dignified presence to the world.

Self-belief seems to radiate from winners. They are confident and walk tall. Their very manner lets people know "I am a good person. I deserve to be respected."

Not everyone will agree when it is said that one's appearance is as importance as her attitude. Appearances count a lot in today's society.

Losers don't give much importance to appearance. They make no move to change and want to be accepted as they are.

However it is not what you look like that counts. It is how you feel about your looks that affects your confidence and self-esteem.

To bring out the best in you, it is important that you feel good about yourself, what you are and what you do. You should be happy with yourself. Only then will you radiate the confidence, energy and enthusiasm that form a vital part of success.

If you are not satisfied with yourself, there will be something holding you back from touching the shores of success – a low self-esteem.

If you carry a good-feeling about yourself you believe that others also will like you the way you are. If you project the image that you are likeable, obviously people will like you.

In short, it is impossible for you to feel confident and assured unless you love and respect yourself.

A healthy self-image along with the associated feelings of competence, confidence and worth is essential to impress a positive image of yourself on others.

The feel good factor

Let us first of all understand what the 'feel good factor' is.
Have you ever had a bad hair day?

A time when, no matter what you do to it, the damn thing will not go into place?

You comb it, brush it and dampen it – all to no avail.

It remains as stubborn as ever.

Now, think back. What was your mood like later? How did you feel that whole day?

Down?
Low on confidence?
Short of self-esteem?

Another question for you.

Think of a complete opposite situation to the 'bad-hair day'.

A time when you've just had your hair done

Or

Just bought a new suit

How do you feel then?

Confident?
A million dollars?
Ready to take on anything?

The feel good factor is such a positive force that it can influence your whole life.

Now suppose that on the very day that you are low and irritated you are called into the Managing Director's office. This comes as a rare chance for you to impress the most important person in the organization and somehow it had to come just at a time when your confidence is not at its best.

Will this help or hinder your performance?

Beyond doubt, hinder!

Erase this image of yourself. Now think of a time when you are wearing one of your favorite suits, your hair is perfectly set and you are feeling confident and sharp and your energy levels are high.

What if you get the call to the M.D's office now? Wouldn't you grab the opportunity to prove yourself? Brimming with confidence, as you would be, nothing will be difficult for you!

So what do you infer?

You must put yourself in a position where you feel confident that you can take on anything to maximize your potential in life.

If you are not happy with your appearance and the things around you, your self-esteem and confidence are affected. The two of them are some of the most important things that determine your performance.

The feel good factor and the feel bad factor are millions of miles apart from each other. What goes without saying is that you must try to inculcate the feel good factor in your life.

How to get it into your life is something that only you will know, as it concerns your life. It will give you that great confidence to perform and excel in everything that you do. And if you do have this factor, success will be handed to you on a plate.

We have already seen what the pros and cons of self-esteem, both high and low, are.

You will in the coming pages see some techniques that will help you boost your self-esteem level and confidence.

In the end, hopefully you will have a better perception of yourself and a good idea of the areas that you have to improve on.

RAISING YOUR SELF-ESTEEM

First of all let us try to get an idea about how you think other people perceive you. In the space provided complete the sentence below with one or two paragraphs. Be as honest as you can:

When a person sees or meets me for the first time they think...

```
┌─────────────────────────────────────────────┐
│                                             │
│                                             │
│                                             │
│                                             │
│                                             │
└─────────────────────────────────────────────┘
```

Complete this sentence with a couple of paragraphs.

When a person sees or meets me for the first time I would like them to think that...

```
┌─────────────────────────────────────────────┐
│                                             │
│                                             │
│                                             │
│                                             │
│                                             │
└─────────────────────────────────────────────┘
```

These are two critical questions that bring to light couple of facts about you – how you think others perceive you and how you want them to perceive you.

Look at what you have written above. If what you want others to think about you and what you feel they presently think about you are the same, then it's a real good sign! That would mean you are what you want to be and people perceive you the way you want to be perceived.

That denotes an extremely high self-esteem.

Now if this is not the case, there are differences between the two, then there are areas that you need to work on. Your self-esteem would have to be given that extra lift.

Write down below the differences that you found between what you feel others think about you and what you feel they think. Also make a brief statement of how you can improve them.

* _____
* _____
* _____
* _____
* _____
* _____
* _____
* _____
* _____
* _____

Some cases would require significant improvements. It may require a diet, exercise and/or grooming. Other minor improvements that some people could do with are in the way they shake hands with others and their ability to remember names.

Now please write down all those characteristics of the person you consider as the ideal person and whom you would like to become like.

Write down below everything about this person. The looks, the hair, the kind of clothes she wears, mannerisms, her car, etc. Don't miss out on any detail, no matter how small it may be.

Done the exercise?

Now ask yourself this question.

Do you prefer her life to your own?

If you do, start to write down what you can do to close the gap:

```
┌─────────────────────────────────────────────────────────┐
│                                                         │
│                                                         │
│                                                         │
│                                                         │
│                                                         │
└─────────────────────────────────────────────────────────┘
```

Regularly doing this exercise will enable your development as a person and will ensure that you will not be distracted from.

No matter what your list says, let us now look at some of the most common areas of personal development. They may not comply to you now but will surely help you in one way or the other in life.

We have already seen how important the feel good factor is in one's life.

To enhance this factor, begin with examining every area of your appearance.

You could perhaps buy an image consultancy book that includes such things as the types and shades of clothing that complement your face and complexion, the hairdo that would bring out the best in your facial features, the most appropriate frame for your glasses to suit your face.

Image consultancy books act as the perfect guide to feeling and looking your best with style, grooming and wardrobe tips.

They enhance your confidence and make you feel great.

Why, you could take one step further and have an actual image consultation.

Looks apart, your possessions are another area that influence your self-esteem.

What you can do is produce a list once a month of the possessions that you would like to have. The contents of the list can be further broken down into three.

The example below would give you a better idea.

1. Items that I can go out and purchase immediately:
E.g. a hat, dress, shoes

2. Items to buy which I would have to save a little
a dress, a computer, a dining set

3. Items that require long term savings
E.g. a car, a house, a luxury vacation

Medium and long term savings plans can then be created to acquire the items listed in 2 and 3 above. Meanwhile you can treat yourself to at least two items per month that form part of 1.

As a result, the smaller possessions will make you feel good. And when you finally buy the larger possessions that need saving, you feel even better!

You will by now have a good idea of what you have to look like, own and possess in order to feel your best.

You could be the most confident person in the world or the least. But there is room for improvement in everyone's life.

It may sound amusing, but in order to make a positive impact on others you should have a love affair yourself. In short, you should feel good about yourself. Because if you feel so, it is apparent to everyone you meet.

If you feel bad about your shape, physique, clothes, grooming, manner or appearance, it will be much harder for you to remain confident and assured in social situations.

Someone once asked:

If you treated your friends like you treated yourself, would you have any?

You are your own best friend because wherever you go, your best friend goes with you. She is always there with you when you need it. Keep that in mind and remember to be nice to yourself.

The way we treat ourselves has a direct impact on how others will treat us.

The way you treat yourself can work as a means to show others how they should treat you.

Consider this case.

Sandy treats herself really well. Everything about her reflects confidence. She eats in the best of restaurants, she has expensive dresses and makes sure that she is well groomed always.

Thanks to this, whenever her friends know that she is coming to their place, guess what they do!

Yes, they tidy up the house, buy her favorite bottle of wine, etc. This happens only because they know how she treats herself. As she treats herself well, they also tend to treat her the same way.

Become Your Own Best Friend and Everyone Else Will Treat You Like Theirs

We had earlier seen the importance of complimenting other people. It is equally important to put yourself in the position whereby you receive the compliments.

Look at yourself.

Are you happy with the way you dress? If yes, then it's great!

But if you are not happy, buy the clothes that you feel will make you feel good.

What about other things - your house, your car, garage and office desk? Are they in a mess? Well then, tidy them up.

You wonder what that has got to do with self-esteem. Fair question.

Okay, think about this.

What if someone new got into your car and there were papers, cans, grit and other stuff lying around? What do you think this says about your self-esteem?

Not anything good, definitely!

Are you happy with your weight? If yes, that's good for you. People like you are a very rare find.

But if you aren't happy, go on an exercise and healthy eating plan.

MAKE PEOPLE SAY

"WOW! YOU LOOK GREAT!"

So many things depend on the level of your self-esteem. It is one thing that can either open many doors for you or shut them tight.

When it comes to those few moments of truth in your life - that 20 minute promotion presentation or that 10 minute chat to the M.D, you must be at your best and feel your best so that you can perform your best.

When you are feeling good about yourself, you feel you can conquer anything. It is a time when no obstacle is too great and no mountain is too steep to climb, for you.

Your self esteem can be improved by internal (thoughts about yourself) and external (appearance, possessions) factors.

To maximize your potential in life you must analyze your SELF-ESTEEM.

Try to put yourself in a position where both your mind and body are one. And remain there.

Once you have achieved this you will know because you will never have felt anything like it - THE POWER OF A HIGH SELF-ESTEEM AND THE CONFIDENCE TO ACHIEVE ALMOST ANYTHING.

So that's it!

Thanks for your continued support.

Remember what you learned. Work out what you want, how you want it and how you will get it and then decide what kind of a person you need to become to get it!

Success is all about common sense, but unfortunately, common sense is not common.

Live life, love often!

Charlotte

Business

Plan Your Best Year Ever With Confidence

As every small business woman knows, if you're not having fun and enjoying your work, it's tough to stay motivated. And if you're not feeling motivated, it's nearly impossible to grow.

So many solo woman entrepreneurs simply exist, working hard day after day, without ever loving their business, and sometimes even coming to resent the very things you used to enjoy.

Or maybe you still look forward to your day-to-day tasks, but have trouble achieving your goals—or even knowing what your goals are. Business feels boring or stagnated, and you can't seem to reach that next level.

Whatever level you're at, whether you're in love with your business today or not, the only sure-fire way to make the next year your best ever is to spend some time reviewing your wins, setting new goals, and planning your strategy for the coming months. If that sounds overwhelming, don't worry. It's easy, and even fun.

REVIEW & CELEBRATE THE PAST 12 MONTHS

Before you can look forward, spend some time looking back. As one vintage ad proclaims, "You've come a long way, baby!" It's time to celebrate! You have very likely accomplished a lot in the past 12 months, even if some days it doesn't feel like it.

Think back to how you started the past year, and make a list of how you've grown and improved.

Keep the following life and business areas in mind as you make your list:
- Family & Relationships
- Financial
- Reputation
- Audience Reach

- Charity & Volunteer Work
- Business Vision
- Spirituality

Then write down where you were then versus where you are now for each of these areas, and any others that are important to you.

THEN	NOW

To-Do:

To make this exercise easier next year, set yourself up right from the start.

1. Create a business diary. This can be as simple as a Google calendar or a notebook in your Evernote with a new note for each day or week. Spend a minute or two at the end of every day and jot down anything you might want to remember later. For example, you might make a note about being published in Huffington Post, or getting re-tweeted by Marie Forleo.

   You may also want to include things like product launch dates and results, affiliate promotions, ad campaigns and how they perform, and anything else you'll want to remember or reference later.

2. Create a "yay me" file. Here is where you'll record all the good stuff. Glowing emails from clients, exceptional reviews, and even particularly flattering photos should be saved and pulled out whenever you need a pick-me-up.

   There are lots of ways to build this file, but don't be afraid to get creative. A fun scrapbook with plenty of color will lift your spirits every time you see it.

UNDERSTANDING YOUR 'WHY'

Before you can set goals or achieve anything in your business or your life, you have to understand what really drives you. What is it that truly gets you up in the morning when all you want to do is roll over and go back to sleep? What forces you to pick up the phone to call yet another potential client? What keeps you going, even when you want to give up?

Your "why" is personal. It's yours alone, and no two why's are exactly alike. More importantly, there's no right or wrong "why."

Perhaps you already know what your why is. Maybe you want to help single moms make a better life for themselves. Maybe you want to earn enough money to retire at 50 and travel the world. You might want to start a cat rescue, spend more time with your kids, or go on a mission trip to Africa. Maybe you just want to make a million dollars.

Once you know what drives you, every decision becomes easier, so before you start setting goals for next year, let's spend some time thinking about why you do what you do.

Answer the following questions:

If money and time were of no concern, what would I do with my days?

Looking back at my past year, what events or accomplishments made my heart light up?

If I lost everything tomorrow, what would I most miss?

If I could trade lives with anyone, who would it be and why?

With these answers in mind, spend at least an hour writing out why you do what you do. *(This is not an easy exercise, and not one that can be rushed, so please take your time.)*

YOUR BUSINESS VISION

You started your business with a vision in mind. You probably daydreamed about what it would look like as you sat in your day-job office waiting for the clock to tell you it was finally time to go home. Maybe you fantasized about how it would be to work from home as you scraped ice off your car in preparation for yet another cold commute in bumper-to-bumper traffic.

What did it look like, this dream business of yours? How did your ideal days roll out? Where did you spend your down time?

Chances are your vision has changed, but you very likely still have a dream of what you want your business—and your life—to look like.

Spend a few minutes and write out (in as much detail as you can) your short and long-term business and life vision.

1 year:

_____

5 years:

_____

10 years:

_____

GOAL SETTING

Now that you know what you want your business and your life to look like, and more importantly, *why*, it's time to set some goals to help you get there. When setting your goals, keep the S.M.A.R.T. model in mind.

Goals should be:
- ➢ **S**pecific
- ➢ **M**easureable
- ➢ **A**chievable
- ➢ **R**esults focused
- ➢ **T**ime-bound

For example, you might set a goal to earn $200,000 (specific, measureable and results focused) in 2016 (time-bound). If your earnings in 2015 were $150,000, then your goal certainly meets the achievable requirement as well, making this a good (SMART) goal.

While "smart" goals are safe and expected, there's something to be said for dreaming big, too. What if you took your "smart" goal of adding $10,000 to your income, and followed Ann Sieg's advice and multiplied that by 10?

In ***"Ecommerce University Business Model" Sieg*** makes the case that the only way to really achieve greatness is to dream bigger and push yourself further by setting goals.

Try setting at least one goal in each of these areas, and don't be afraid to take your initial goal and multiply it by 10:

Family & Relationships

Financial

Spiritual

Charity & Volunteer Work

Business Growth

BREAKING IT DOWN: YOUR YEAR AT A GLANCE

Now that you know what your goals are, it's time to break them down into manageable chunks. It's much easier to think about adding 100 people to your mailing list this week than it is to consider the monumental task of adding 5,000 people this year.

Use the table below to break your big goals into smaller, more manageable pieces.

YEARLY GOAL	MONTHLY GOAL	WEEKLY GOAL

CREATE DO-ABLE TASKS

Reaching your goals won't just happen. You have to put in the work in order to achieve new heights.

You've already broken your goals down into monthly and weekly milestones, so now it's time to plan the tasks to reach those milestones. For example, if you set a goal of adding 100 people to your mailing list each week, and you know that your landing page converts at 20%, then you need to drive 500 new people to your page.

You might do that by running paid Facebook ads, sharing your URL on Twitter and LinkedIn, or buying solo ads. (In each case, you'll need to test and track to ensure you're spending and sharing in the correct numbers to reach your goal.)

WEEKLY GOAL	TASK TO ACHIEVE	TASK TO ACHIEVE

RESOURCES I NEED

No business—or life—operates in a vacuum. You need help. People, tools and training are all critical to your success. Some examples of necessary resources include:

Business Tools
- Web hosting
- Mailing list manager
- Shopping cart
- Social media presence
- Landing page creator
- Webinar host

Business Training
- Email marketing & list building
- Facebook ads
- Blogging/content marketing
- Technology training

People
- JV Partners and affiliates
- Virtual assistants
- Copywriters
- Graphic designers
- Video/audio editors

When you think of your goals and vision for the coming year, make a note about the resources needed to accomplish those goals. Some of them you likely already have, some you will need to research and add to your current list.

What's missing from my business and life that will help me achieve my goals?

ACCOUNTABILITY & SUPPORT

Aside from the tools and training you'll need to achieve your goals, you'll very likely need support and accountability from others as well.

Who will keep you motivated when you just want to give up?
Who will help increase conversions on your landing pages?
Who will share different ideas and perspectives with you to help increase sales?
As a small business owner, you need a solid support system to help you get the right things done.

These support people will include:
- Your spouse or significant other
- Your business partner (if you have one)
- Your mastermind group
- Your accountability partner
- Your business and/or life coach

Which of these do you currently have? Which do you need? What roles will they fill in your goal setting and business growth?

PERSON	ROLE

A LIVING DOCUMENT

The goals and task lists you've created are only the beginning. You'll continue to add to them as new ideas occur, and old ones turn out not to work (or you hate doing them, or they've lost their importance).

So don't look at any of these as a MUST do list. Look at them as a CAN do list instead.

Here's the really important thing, though: Do something every day. Pick one thing that will move you closer toward your goals each and every day, and once in a while—say once per quarter—revisit your goals and your vision and ask yourself, "Is this still what I really want from life?"

Then make your decisions with confidence accordingly.

To your success,

Charlotte Howard

DISCOVER MORE
ABOUT CONTRIBUTING AUTHORS

Charlotte Howard

Daija Howard

Sharon Nicholas

Sonya Davis

Heart Centered Women Media, is seeking more amazing women to feature in upcoming inspirational books, anthologies and events?

Contact Charlotte Howard at 803-414-2117 or www.HeartCenteredWomenMedia.com to be considered.

www.ingramcontent.com/pod-product-compliance
Lightning Source LLC
Chambersburg PA
CBHW070817100426
42742CB00012B/2383